P9-DMQ-149

GOLD! GOLD!

A Beginners Handbook and Recreational Guide:
How and Where To Prospect For Gold!

J. F. Petralia

Gold! Gold!

A beginner's handbook and recreational guide:
How and Where to prospect for gold!
Copyright © 1980 by Joseph F. Petralia
2nd.Revised Copyright © 1999 by Joseph F. Petralia
Copyright © 2006 by Joseph F. Petralia

All rights reserved. No part of this book may be reproduced in
any form or by any means, electronic, mechanical or otherwise,
including information storage and retrieval systems, without
the express permission in writing from the publisher, except by
a reviewer, who may quote brief passages in a review.

Design by Carol Hoover
Drawings by Susan Neri
Typesetting by Type by Design
Editorial Assistance by Jill Applegate
Contemporary photos By author
Cover art Copyright © 1982
by Sierra Outdoor Products Co.®

Acknowledgments: Nineteenth Century photographs
and sketches courtesy of:

> *Levi Strauss & Co.*
> *The Bancroft Library, U.C. Berkeley*
> *Wells Fargo Bank History Room*
> *California Division of Mines and Geology*
> *Southern Pacific Transportation Co.*
> *Federal Reserve Bank of San Francisco*
> *Old Mint Museum, San Francisco*

Published By:
Sierra Outdoor Products Co.®
P.O. Box 2497
San Francisco, CA 94126-2497
http://www.sierraoutdoorproducts.com

Library of Congress Catalog Card Number: 81-126200

Library of Congress Catalog-In-Publication Data

Gold! Gold! / Joseph F. Petralia

ISBN 978-0-9605890-0-5 Softcover Edition

Printed in the United States of America 2007

Dedicated to all those whose love of the great outdoors and lure of the past will be expanded in this new hobby.

Hardrock miners at Virginia City Comstock Lode wearing their "Levi's." *(Photo courtesy of Levi Strauss & Co.)*

Contents

CHAPTER I

In the Beginning . . .

Throughout history the story of mankind and the mention of gold have been closely intertwined. It is almost universally considered to be the symbol of everything that is precious and of enduring value, thereby creating its role as a store of value for individuals and entire nations. The form that it has taken has been multi-faceted: from nuggets, ingots, coins, and idols to the current coin mintage of various countries around the world. It has been highly prized for its own attractive nature as well as its ability to withstand the rigors of time. It has been considered dear both because of the effort required to extract it from nature and its scarcity relative to the other metals of the earth.

Mankind has valued gold since the beginning of civilization. The ancient Egyptians were fashioning artifacts from gold as far back as 4000 B.C. and it is the first element mentioned in the Bible (Genesis 2: 10–12).

> A river flowed out of Eden to water the garden, and there it divided and became four rivers. The name of the first is Pishon; it is the one which flows around the whole land of Havilah, where there is gold, and the gold of that land is good.

Although gold was somewhat scarce in early times, there was enough available to be used in

Down the Sierra Nevadas in 1865
(Courtesy of Wells Fargo Bank)

9

both daily transactions and as a medium of exchange. It's been the natural way for man to preserve capital and the fruits of his labor as well as a way to protect him from monetary debasement and uncertainty. It has been continually sought since ancient times, plundered from the ancient civilizations of the Inca and the Aztec, and the primary mover in the westward development of this country. Its recent domestic extraction includes several recent gold rushes, beginning in the early 19th century in the southeastern United States, followed by the great California rush of 1849/50 and by later strikes in the Rockies and Alaska. In spite of this pressure, it is estimated that over 80% of all gold still existing worldwide has not yet been recovered.

The King of Money

In more recent times, gold has been used as a hedge against inflation, particularly in countries outside of the United States. The "hoarding" of various bullion pieces (Napolean Francs, Kruggerands, U.S. Double Eagles) is most prevalent during periods of adverse world conditions and economic uncertainty.

(Courtesy Federal Reserve Bank, San Francisco)

Gold – the ultimate money – Why? Because it is the only monetary asset that isn't someone else's liability. It doesn't represent a promise to pay and it isn't dependent upon the survival of a particular power or group of powers. In a word, it is valuable because it is.

How To Wheel and Deal in Gold and Silver. C. M. Allen. 1974.

Gold: Its Nature

Gold is unique among the metals and is considered noble and beautiful by many people. Among its unique physical properties, gold is the most malleable and ductile of all metals, with the ability to be stretched or drawn. It has been estimated that a single ounce of gold can be drawn into a wire over 40 miles long without breaking. It is also an extremely dense metal having a specific gravity of 19.2 (19 times heavier than water). Gold is an excellent conductor of electricity. Its "nobility" means that no substance that appears commonly in nature will destroy it. It is virtually immune to the effects of oxygen and therefore will not corrode, tarnish, or rust. Caches of coins unearthed after centuries from both sea and land have been recovered as brilliant as the day they were lost.

Besides its physical properties, its luster and deep yellow color have, since its initial discovery, lured men and women with an attraction beyond rational comprehension. It is said that if you stare at gold long enough it begins to glow with an iridescence of its own, drawing the observer into its aura. Many have succumbed to what is commonly referred to as "gold fever."

From 1933 until December 31, 1974, it was illegal for Americans to own gold bullion in the United States. Exceptions to this included certain coins which were considered to be of numismatic

Sutter's Mill

quality and gold in its natural state. The ending of the 41-year ban started among Americans a boom in ownership of gold in its various forms. The anticipation of its legalization toward the end of 1974 caused the price of gold to rise steadily, in part buoyed by foreign speculators waiting for Americans to cash in on their new-found freedom. Subsequent leveling of the market price in the ensuing months left some disappointed with its performance. The artificial rise dissipated and gave way to the increasing pressures of the market place. The economic policies of world governments have brought the price of gold up to its current levels. It has been anticipated that its rightful place in today's dollars is over the $1000 mark, which should be reached by the mid-point in this decade. World events, however, could push the price above this level in a matter of weeks. It is obvious that the opening of this new decade will give birth to a new gold rush which brings us to the subject of this book, namely, how to participate and recover your share of "free" gold as it exists in nature.

Gold Fever!

The so-called rush of '49 began with the discovery in 1848 by James W. Marshall on land recently acquired by John C. Fremont. Captain Sutter, a Swiss immigrant, founded the first inland settlement in northern California and built a fort in what is now Sacramento. Later Sutter contracted Marshall to build a sawmill to assure himself of a steady supply of lumber to continue the expansion and settlement of the interior of California.

In January of that year a dam and race (channel) were built on the American River.

For four months these men washed at Coloma, seeing no visitors, and rarely communi-

Sutter's Mill—site of the 1848 discovery of gold in California. *(Courtesy, The Bancroft Library.)*

cating with the fort. The Mill had been nearly completed, the dam was made, the race had been dug, the gates had been put in place, the water had been turned into the race to carry away some of the loose dirt and gravel, and then had been turned off again. On the afternoon of Monday the 24th of January, Marshall was walking in the tail-race, when on its rotten granite bedrock he saw yellow particles and picked up several of them. The largest were about the size of grains of wheat. They were smooth, bright, and in color much like brass. He thought they were gold, and went to the mill, where he told the men that he had found a gold mine. At the time little importance was attached to this statement. It was regarded as a proper subject for ridicule.

Century Magazine, The Century Co., New York. Nov. 1890–April 1891.

Since none of these men had any extensive background in mining, they were neither very excited nor even sure that the "yellow stuff" he had picked up was gold.

Marshall hammered his new metal, and found it malleable; he put it in the kitchen fire, and observed that it did not readily melt or become colored; he compared its color with gold coin; and the more he examined it, the more he was convinced that it was gold.

Century Magazine, The Century Co., New York. Nov. 1890–April 1891.

Captain Sutter was informed of the discovery later that day and performed his own tests. Convinced, but anxious to complete several building projects he had started, he asked that the news be kept secret for several weeks, but to no avail. Sutter, prior to being fully satisfied about the nature of the discovery, had made certain treaties with local Indians, buying their title to the region around the mill in the event their find proved good. Only the remoteness of the sawmill slowed the swift spread of news about the discovery.

The following month Sutter went to the settlement of Yerba Buena (San Francisco), taking samples of the element with him. While in San Francisco he met Issac Humphrey, an old Georgian miner who examined the pieces and confirmed that he had discovered gold in what would later prove to be very rich diggings. Humphrey outfitted a small expedition which reached the site of Sutter's mill in March, 1848. There he made a "rocker" and commenced work in earnest. After several days prospecting the area, he confirmed that the area was, in fact, rich. The first reports were published in two San Francisco newspapers soon thereafter.

Over the next few weeks and months word of their success continued to reach and excite the civilized world. Young and old were seized by the prospect of picking up a fortune for the seeking of it. Representatives of thousands of families back east and overseas were "grub-staked" to make their fortunes for their families. Coloma, the site of Sutter's mill, became California's first mining camp.[*]

The Rush had begun!

The migration to the mountains began with those already in the province, from the settlements in San Francisco and Sonoma, Monterey, San Jose, Santa Cruz, and as word spread, from the communities in the south. As word reached across the Pacific, vessels loaded with fortune-seekers began arriving from the Hawaiian Islands, from posts in the northwest, and eventually strong interest developed on the east coast.

Some immigrants took the southern route around the Horn, other adventurers forming partnerships and companies, travelled overland to the rich mountain streams of the Sierra. The journey was bewilderingly harder than most could imagine,

15

*See Appendix, Page 129

and many had to wait weeks for a craft to round the Horn before proceeding to San Francisco. Hundreds could only afford the voyage in steerage class, and some contracted the fevers of the tropical regions never to reach the Pacific shore. The overland immigrants had to suffer the rigors of the elements and the Indians; those departing too late never made it over the winter mountain passes.

The scene upon arrival in San Francisco was one of various languages, talents, and backgrounds of merchants, commoners, and soldiers, most under-equipped and under-supplied but of one common purpose. Most had arrived too late to get into the mountains to do any good that year. The ground swell of news coming from the earlier arrivals out of the mountains served only to excite further those who were waiting. The true rush was to begin in the Spring of 1849.

Early argonauts join in the "rush." *(Courtesy of The California Historical Society, San Francisco)*

Living in San Francisco during that winter was expensive because of the numbers of men and the scarcity of supplies. However, where work was available, the pay was high, and payment prompt. This did little to temper the excitement of the time. The impression was that the gold fields would be exhausted in a year or two, and it would behoove those who expected to gain much to be among the earliest in the fields. There was little background for most of the men in this type of experiment and the various patent mining contrivances they had brought with them had to be replaced with the pick, shovel, and pan before they were to depart.

> In 1848 the gold hunters didn't need a scientific education. The method of washing gold was then so simple — with the savings of a week's work he could buy the pick, shovel, pan and rocker which were the only necessary tools. The auriferous deposits of the Sierra Nevada was done on the bars of rivers, where the gravel was shallow and rich.
> *Miners Own Book, San Francisco, Published by Hutchings and Rosenfield, 146 Montgomery Street.*

The stereotype of the gold rush was born in the fall of '49 and the spring of '50. Times were free and easy. Most had left both their families and the restraints of contemporary society behind them. It was a generation of bachelors, their families several mountain ranges away. Gambling houses abounded with displays of gold dust, nuggets, and "slugs." The streets were filled with men arriving daily with their pouches full. They parted with the gold freely, as men can when it is easily obtained.

> . . . the testimony of the miniature rocks; the solid nuggets brought down from above every few days, whose size and value rumor multiplied according to the number of her tongues. The talk,

day and night, unceasingly and exclusively of "gold, easy to get and hard to hold," inflamed all new comers with the desire to hurry on and share the chances.

History of Marin County; Historical Sketch of the State of California. Alley, Bowen & Co., 1880.

The Fever Spreads!

As word of new discoveries became known, more and more people caught the "fever."

The discovery of these vast deposits of gold has entirely changed the character of upper California. Its people, before engaged in cultivating their small patches of ground, and guarding their herds of cattle and horses, have all gone to the mines, or are on their way there. Labourers of every trade have left their work-benches, and tradesmen their shops. Sailors desert their ships as fast as they arrive on the coast . . . many desertions, too, have taken place from the garrison within the influence of these mines.

At present the people are running over the county and picking it out of the earth here and there, just as a thousand hogs, let loose in the forest, would root up grounds-nuts. Some get eight or ten ounces a day, and the least active one or two.

Guide to the Gold Region of Upper California by William Thurston esq. 1849.

It's possible that a 20th century version of this experience will be relived as the price of gold climbs over the $500.00/ounce mark.

Mining Life

The method of the day was to work in groups or companies of men extracting the easiest and most accessible gold then moving on to richer grounds once the fertile area was depleted. The general theory was that the richest gold was at the source. Therefore it followed that moving further up the gorges and unexplored streams and creeks

would offer the richest finds. Hence, the development of the various camps and towns along the tributaries of the major gold-producing rivers (Yuba, Tuolomne, Feather, American, etc.).

Early woodcut.
(Courtesy of Wells Fargo Bank History Room)

A turn of the road presented a scene of mining life, as perfect in its details as it was novel in its features. Immediately beneath us the swift river glided tranquilly, though foaming still from the great battle which a few yards higher up it had fought with a mass of black obstructing rocks. On the banks a village of canvas that the winter rains had bleached to perfection, and round it the miners were at work at every point. Many were waist deep in the water, toiling in banks to construct a race and dam to turn the river's course; others were entrenched in holes, like grave diggers, working down to the "bedrock." Some were on the bank of the stream washing out "prospects" from tin pans and wooden "bateas"; and others working in company with the long tom, by means of water sluices artfully conveyed from the river. Many were coyoteing in subterranean holes, from which time to time their heads popped out, like those of squirrels to take a look at the world; and a few with drills, dissatisfied with nature's work, were preparing to remove large rocks with gunpowder. All was life, merriment, vigor and determination, as their part of the earth was being turned inside out to see what it was made of.

Marryat, Frank, Mountain-Molehills, London. 1855. p. 234.

The Motherlode

The gold regions of California are generally broken up into three categories: the so-called northern, the central, and the southern district mines (see map). For the most part, these districts parallel the main north-south road through the "mother lode" area named after the region bearing the most extensive concentration of gold.

Highway 49 runs north and south through California in the central Sierras from approximately Mariposa at the southern boundary to Sierra City in the north, a distance of over 175 miles. Colorful towns, whose names stir images of the past, appeared, such as Angel's Camp, Fiddletown, Columbia, Auburn, Rough and Ready, and countless others whose lifetime did not exceed several weeks. Towns sprang up like mushrooms after a spring rain, some with equal longevity. Most of the 'camps' consisted of little more than a series of tents or cabins that were only slightly more durable.

Travelling through the various towns today offers a rich experience and insight into the history

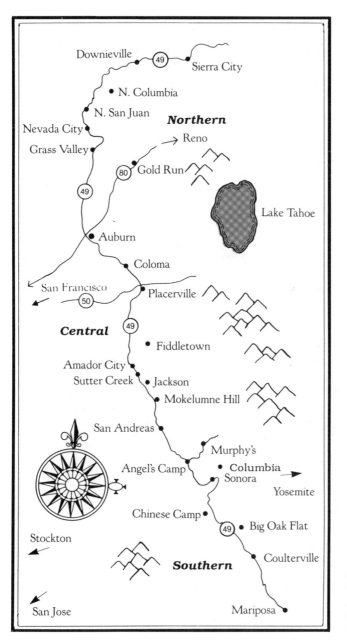

Downieville 49 Sierra City

• N. Columbia

N. San Juan

Northern

Nevada City

→ Reno

Grass Valley

80 Gold Run

49

Lake Tahoe

• Auburn

Coloma

San Francisco

Placerville

50

Central 49

• Fiddletown

Amador City

Sutter Creek • Jackson

• Mokelumne Hill

San Andreas

Murphy's

Angel's Camp • Columbia
Sonora

Yosemite

Chinese Camp •

49 • Big Oak Flat

Stockton

Coulterville

Southern

San Jose

Mariposa •

California's "Mother Lode": Route 49 named after the "forty-niners."

of several generations of our past. Many of the towns along Highway 49 are well-preserved. However, many of the lesser-populated and uncommercialized settlements are on side roads easily reached by the family car.

CHAPTER II

The Pot at the End of the Rainbow

T he expression "Gold is where you find it" has been used by generations of prospectors. The reasoning is simple: although there would seem to be technical and physical reasons for recovering gold from the place it should logically rest, that's not always the case.

> Of all metals, gold is, with the exception of iron, the most widely distributed over the earth; but it differs from the latter metal in being present usually in a nearly pure state, but in exceedingly small quantities, whereas iron is abundant as well as generally diffused and is never found unmixed with other substances. Owing to the very minute proportion in which gold is often associated with rocks and mineral substances, it does not generally pay the cost of working; and the districts therefore known as "auriferous" or "gold-producing," in the commercial sense of the term, are not so numerous as the fore-going remarks might seem to suggest.
> *The Gold Seeker's Manual by David T. Anstead, Professor of Biology, Kings College, London. 1849.*

As noted, gold is found in most areas of the world in various forms. The leading commercial producer is South Africa, followed by the Soviet Union, Canada, and the United States. It is found in the mountains, the desert, and in the sea, where it is estimated that six parts of gold are found for

◄——
Twentieth Century "Miners": Author (left) working claim on the North Fork of the Yuba River.

every trillion parts of salt water. Obviously, in this case, its recovery value is lost unless an economical means of obtaining it is perfected. For the purposes of this handbook, we'll limit ourselves to those areas and methods which you will more than likely use.

The most abundant areas for gold in the United States are located in the Sierra Nevada and Rocky Mountain ranges. However, there have been sufficient concentrations of gold in the southeastern United States (mined during 1830–1840), in the Appalachian Mountains, and in the mountainous regions of Vermont and New Hampshire to warrant increasing interest at the current price levels. Some of the more outstanding states for prospecting include California, Colorado, South Dakota, Alaska, Nevada, Utah, Montana, Idaho, Washington, Arkansas, New Mexico, Wyoming, North and South Carolina, and Georgia.

To better understand where to find gold we should first re-examine its nature. The weight of gold concerns us most. One of nature's heaviest metals, with an atomic weight of 196.967, gold is extremely dense. A cubic foot of gold weighs more than one-half ton, and at $500 an ounce, it would be worth over $9 million. With this in mind, let's look at some of the most likely areas for prospecting.

Where to Begin Your Search

For all intents and purposes, those areas that have produced the best in the past will be the most likely to continue producing. Therefore, we should begin our research with the various public information bureaus for records of recovery in earlier years. The local Bureau of Land Management (BLM) regional office has a number of publications outlining specific areas within your state and

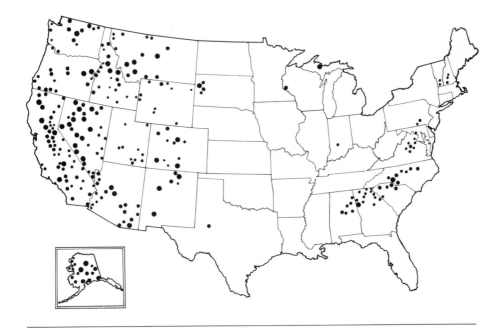

county. This department can be very helpful in supplying both topographical maps (at a nominal fee) as well as offering reference material on production levels within their jurisdiction. Your local library can also supply a wealth of information on the gold districts within your region. A check at the State Department of Miners and Geology can provide a geological map of the area showing the mineral deposits.

It should be emphasized that there is a tremendous wealth of information available for the asking. In every instance these departments can provide invaluable aid and cheerful assistance in directing you to the information you seek.

Let's go back to basics using California as an example. . . .

In Short . . .

In ancient times, in what is generally accepted as the Jurassic period, the surface of the central part of the state was uplifted and intruded

Known gold concentrations in the United States. (See Chapter VII)

by molten magma from deep within the earth. In the cooling and contracting that followed many cracks and fissures were formed. Gold and other elements were eventually forced into these openings by the intense pressure of rising hot water and residual gaseous solutions. These gold-bearing *veins*, still deep beneath the earth's surface, were exposed by the erosive conditions of the late Cretaceous period that followed. The streams of the subsequent Eocene epoch ran over and through the metamorphic rock and mineralized zones to form and concentrate the placer deposits. The subtropical climate and other conditions of the period were very favorable to continued disintegration of the "host" matrix.

During the ensuing Tertiary Sierran uplift, the rivers ran basically in a north-south direction. However, the tremendous forces within the earth which caused the uplift and tilting of the region interrupted their flow. Through the passage of time new drainage was formed which cut through the older channels and released the gold deposits. These relatively new watercourses running perpendicular (east-west) to the older Tertiary

The Mexican 'Rastre. Sketch from Hutchings' California Magazine, 1857.

channels are the gold-rich rivers and streams that started all the excitement over a century ago.

The Tertiary stream gravels, which had long been buried deeply beneath lavas, were exposed by the Pleistocene canyon-cutting rivers. From the dissected portions of the old channels, gold was removed and washed into the newer streams, which concentrated it on their bedrock riffles. The remaining portions of the Tertiary deposits were left with their stubs exposed high up on the intervening ridges. In places, erosion merely stripped the covering of volcanic tuffs, sands and gravels from the bedrock, leaving the channel with its rich gold deposits laid practically bare for the lucky early miner to win.

Olaf P. Jenkins, Chief, Division of Mines and Geology, Retired. Geology of Placer Deposits. Special Publication 34. p. 27

Where the gold is still held in the host rock, it is known as "lode" gold and its extraction is called "lode" or "hard rock mining." The gold occurs in thin veins formed when it, and often granite or quartz, was in a molten state and subsequently forced up from beneath the earth's crust. Commercial operations first have to tunnel into the mountain, or dig a tunnel or shaft, to extract the "ore," perhaps blasting out the surrounding material. The ore-bearing rock would then be crushed to free the gold, using a mechanical device known as a "stampmill." It operated as its name implies: the stamp acted as a giant pestle, rising and falling by means of a cam driven by a power shaft, and crushing the material being fed to it.

In early operations in the past century the action of an "arrastre" was substituted. This was a large round stone fastened to a horizontal wooden arm. The arm was attached to a large vertical center timber which was embedded in the ground and used as a pivot. The movement of the stone, which crushed the ore, was powered by a mule walking in a circle.

On occasion, particularly when the lower grade ore was eventually mined, the arrastre was used in conjunction with the stampmill to further reduce the material and maximize the return of gold. This type of mining is labor-intensive and its overhead closed down many operations. Recently, some of these mines have been reopened because of the current market price of the precious metal.

Why it is Where it is

During the course of erosion, the weathering action will deteriorate the host material of the veins in a gold-bearing region. The action of rain and runoffs will gradually move the eroded gold,

The deposition of gold as it erodes from source to stream placer.

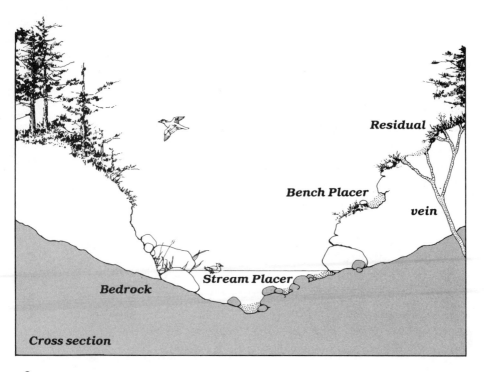

sometimes still clinging to the host-quartz, down the slopes, gullies and drainages of the mountainside. Cumulative deposits will in time come to rest in the nearby creeks and streams. Depending on their location they are classified as either Bench or Stream Placers (illustration).

> In order that a major deposition of gold may occur, there must be an abundance of source material which contains more or less gold and which may be more or less easily eroded. A decayed formation of low-grade material could easily furnish more gold than a hard, higher grade deposit. The decomposed material also supplies more gravel for balanced conditions of stream transportation, providing that overloading or choking is minimized by uplifts or increasing water volume. Plainly, a stream running along a vein system will have a greater opportunity to accumulate gold than one merely crossing it. Bedrock-controlled streams, therefore, provide a maximum contact with source material.
> *Nov. 1934 paper written by Jenkins, O. P. and Wright, W. Q. California gold-bearing Tertiary Channels, Engineering and Mining Journal, Vol. 135, p. 501.*

Types of Deposits

A placer deposit is the formation caused by the natural erosion of lode ore from its original resting place. The heat of summer, the expansion and contraction of surrounding rock and soil, glacier drifts, earthquake faults, winter snows, summer thaws, and subsequent rains, runoffs, and floods all exert pressure to move and break down the gold vein from its point of origin to the resting place where you can recover it.

As noted above, *Bench* and *Stream Placers*, are similar in nature: the former is an ancient deposit of a streambed that has been isolated, i.e., left "high and dry," as the stream eroded its way

deeper into the face of the mountain, or changed direction, stranding the gold above the current water level. These "benches" can be 20 to 100 feet above the river and can usually be spotted by the round "tumbled" river rocks they contain. By visually locating the point at which the bench lies on bedrock and prospecting the material, you'll be working on choice ground.

A Stream Placer, on the other hand, is located within the range of the present level of water. It contains deposits of gold-bearing material either in "gravel bars" (illustration) or other areas, including subsurface, which, for reasons we'll discuss, accumulated the heaviest water-borne elements.

> For the most part, the original source of gold is not far from the place where it was first deposited after being carried by running water.
> Olaf P. Jenkins, "Geology of Placer Deposits," Mineral Information Service, Vol. 17, Nos. 1–9, 1964.

The richest places, however, are not necessarily those closest to the source. This is not a contradiction. The formation of the placer deposits is heavily dependent upon how the placer material is rewashed by natural forces to concentrate the amount of recoverable gold. I'll elaborate further a little later on.

The *Placer* gold we're after is gold in its natural or raw state. It can be found in sizes ranging from finest "flour" to substantial "nuggets" washed or dredged from either active or dry streambeds. Since placer gold is alloyed in nature with other native elements, its purity will usually vary from 700/1000 to 900/1000 fine.

Let's assume that you have researched the various materials available from the Bureau of Land Management, Bureau of Mines, local history from your library, etc., and are now surveying a

◄

River in late summer. Note formation of "gravel bar" on left bank.

particular area. The easiest method for taking in the greatest land area is the topographical map. If you were to zero in on a specific area in the mountains of Georgia, or a river in Colorado, or a stream in Canada, you would be able to purchase from either the BLM or a large map store, the topographical map covering your particular locality. By doing so, you would have a bird's-eye view of the area that would enable you to study the meandering direction of streams, land contour, and stream gradient. What you should be looking for are areas in streams where gold, during its movement, would become trapped.

Let's review a few places you are likely to encounter deposits in your prospecting. A *Residual* or "primary" deposit is one which occurs at the surface of the ground or at the origin or outcropping of a gold vein which has eroded. In order for gold to be released from its original source in bedrock, the encasing matrix (host material) must be broken down through weathering, glacial action, faulting, uplift, chemical disintegration, etc.

> On its way down the hillside gold is sometimes concentrated in sufficient amounts to warrant mining. Such deposits are classified as *Eluvial* placers—they are transitional between residual and stream, or *Alluvial* deposits.
> *Olaf P. Jenkins, "Geology of Placer Deposits," Mineral Information Service, Vol. 17, Nos. 1–9, 1964.*

The secondary types of deposits are "transported" placers and are classified by their distance from their source and location. Therefore a *Eluvial* deposit is one which has moved a short distance from its original location.

Imagine, if you will, the movement from a residual deposit as it travels down the face of a weathering mountain to a stream. Picture a vein of pure gold an inch or so in diameter and several feet long just under the surface of the soil. If you were prospecting electronically, with the aid of a metal detector, and chanced upon the discovery of this vein, in its original location, you would have discovered lode gold. If this gold had eroded, the immediate area would be a residual deposit.

Eventually the placer gold we are looking for will work its way down in the gullies, creeks, streams, and rivers that drain these mountain regions. The type and texture of the underlying rock structures of these waterways will determine the retaining ability of each area.

> A further and very important factor is the ability of the bedrock to hold the deposited gold in spite of the scouring action of the stream at higher water stages. A smooth, hard bedrock is a very poor one for placer accumulations. Bedrock formations which are decomposed or possess cracks and crevices are good, and those of a clayey or a schistose nature are excellent in their ability to retain particles of gold.
> *Nov. 1934 paper by Jenkins, O. P., and Wright, W. Q. California gold-bearing tertiary Channels, Engineering and Mining Journal, Vol. 135, p. 501.*

River/stream bottoms which have been displaced to form a "ledge" perpendicular to the direction of the stream can provide an excellent subsurface pocket for accumulation of gold.

Its "Heft" is the Main Clue

Gold, being heavier than any other materials you are likely to find, will be moving very reluctantly in the watercourse of the stream. In doing so, it will generally move in a straight line following the path of least resistance and taking the shortest distance between two points in the stream course.

Bearing these images in mind, let us proceed again to look for a likely place to make our discovery.

One way to approach the study of the topographical map is to look for areas where the stream or river will be making a sharp turn. Gold, moving from its original point of deposit into the stream, will generally move during periods of heavy flooding, high water, spring thaws, or during mountain storms. During this period of heavy water flow there will be several factors that will effect the velocity or speed of the water: namely the stream gradient (the amount of drop or angle of the stream over a particular distance), and the width to contain it. Unless the gold has been freshly deposited, its weight will cause it to quickly settle and embed itself in the various cracks, fissures, roots, and other obstacles in its path as it moves downstream. It will, therefore, take substantial velocity for it to move again (Newton's "object at rest"). Periods of unusually heavy flooding, which occur every few years, tend to rearrange these deposits.

Images: A Nugget's Travels

Imagine standing at a high vantage point during an unusually heavy spring runoff. If you were to drop a relatively large lump of gold, say the size of an almond, in this fast-moving water, how would it travel? If the stream were fast and narrow, with little obstruction, our test lump of gold would probably travel uninterrupted for the full course of the stream. But nature doesn't form streams that are smooth, straight, and narrow. Each turn, new tributary, outcropping, variation in grade, etc., will determine the velocity at each given point.

Again, using the simplified illustration (figure 1), if we were to drop our nugget in a fast-

Figure 1: Boulder or bedrock outcropping at inside bend will cause the formation of a gravel bar – prospect its upstream end.

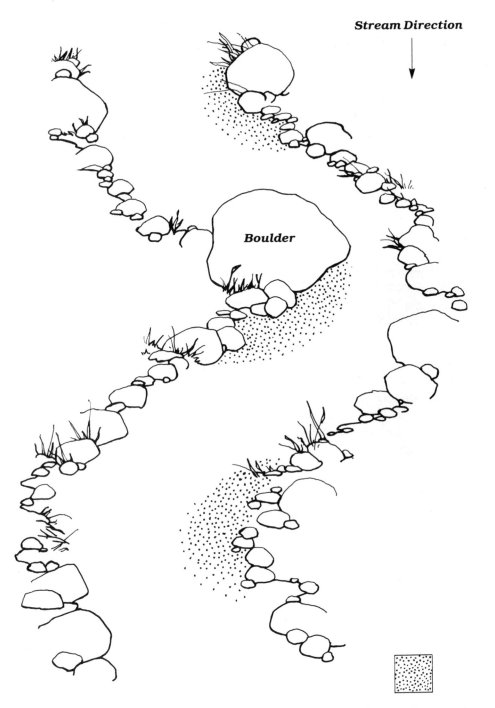

Stream Direction

Boulder

Area to Prospect

35

moving, man-made stream with only one obstruction, such as a large boulder in the middle of that stream, the boulder would have an area of still water or relatively calmer water on its downstream side. In all likelihood our lump of gold would be travelling at a more-or-less constant rate carried along by the force of the water. However, upon reaching and being swept around the boulder, the nugget's weight would most likely cause it to stop and hold its position in the calmer water on the lee side of the boulder, there to rest as the water gradually receded.

Let us take another instance using a straight and narrow hypothetical stream of a fixed grade (figure 2) swelled by a spring runoff. Midway through its course imagine a sharp bend. Several hundred feet above this bend we drop in our test nugget. From our vantage point we see the nugget being swept along down the straight, smooth part of the stream until it reaches the point where the stream begins to make its sharp curve.

In a straight channel the current is swifter near the middle than near the sides and is swifter above mid-depth than below. On arriving at a bend the whole stream resists change of course, but the resistance is more effective for the swifter parts of the stream than for the slower. The upper central part is deflected least and projects itself against the outer bank. In so doing it displaces the slow-flowing water previously near the bank, and that water descends obliquely. The descending water displaces in turn the slow-flowing lower water, which is crowded toward the inner bank, while the water previously near that bank moves toward the middle as an upper layer. One general result is a twisting movement, the upper parts of the current tending toward the outer bank and the lower toward the inner. Another result is that the swiftest current is no longer medial, but is near the outer or concave bank. Connected with these two is a gradation of velocities across the

**Figure 2:
Inside bends have heavier gravel deposits (bars) and often trap gold.**

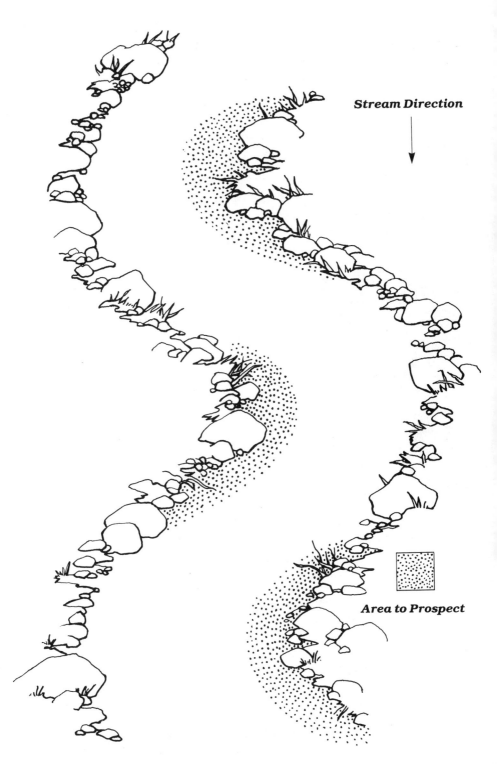

Stream Direction

Area to Prospect

bottom, the greater velocities being near the outer bank. The bed velocities near the outer bank are not only much greater than those near the inner bank but they are greater than any bed velocities in a relatively straight part of the stream. They have therefore greater capacity for traction, and by increasing the tractional lead they erode until an equilibrium is attained. On the other hand, the currents which, crossing the bed obliquely, approach the inner bend are slackening currents, and they deposit what they can no longer carry.

Quoted from G. N. Gilbert, Geology of Placer Deposits, Division of Mines and Geology, SP 34, p. 19.

The water on the *inside* of that curve will be running *slower* than at any other point in the bend, therefore enabling our nugget to resist and settle in the inside curve. Its weight will cause the gold to travel in a straight path following a line of least resistance from inside bend to inside bend.

Another example relating to resistance and deposition of gold would be our stream with equal proportions throughout, but which suddenly increases its width at the midway point (figure 3). Again, our test nugget would travel along quite rapidly, moved by the constant flow of water until it reached the point where the stream widened. The wider point offers the water a chance to slacken, affording the gold an opportunity to settle in the slower water.

The transporting power of a stream is dependent on its velocity, which is a variant determined by the gradient, volume and load. When a stream is overloaded with sediment, the excess is dropped. When it is underloaded, it erodes. When equilibrium has been established, neither erosion nor deposition take place. Gradient, volume and load usually vary in the same stream so that deposition may be going on in one part of its valley and erosion in another.

Figure 3: Placer deposits accumulate in areas where stream velocity is reduced such as in widened areas in streambed, down-stream of rapids.

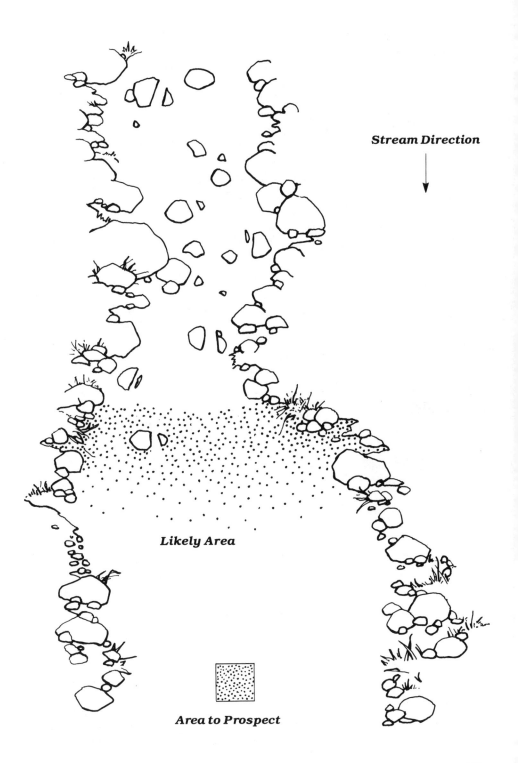

Stream Direction

Likely Area

Area to Prospect

When a stream is eroding, the material within reach of its activity is constantly moved in a downstream direction. All movements of this kind are accomplished by more or less sorting and make for the concentration of the heavier particles.

Deposition takes place in a stream when the velocity is decreased, either by the periodic changes in volume or by a change of gradient. Where there is a change of grade, resulting in diminished velocity, the gold is laid down with the other sediments. It must be remembered, however, that placer gold may find lodgment in inequalities of the bedrock surface where no considerable deposition of detrital matter has taken place, though extensive placers are, as a rule, not formed because of irregularities in the bed-rock surface below. The concentration of gold in river bars is analogous to its deposition in stream beds, for it is dropped where the velocity of the current is checked by the formation of eddies, due to the inequalities of the river floor.

Gold has a specific gravity of approximately six times that of gravel but under water this ratio becomes about nine times. This large gravity difference permits the gold quickly to work its way to bedrock and into crevices.

A. H. Brooks, article on the gold placers of the Seward Peninsula, U.S. Geological Survey Bulletin 328, pp. 125–127.

What we are looking for then, when we study our topological map, aerial photograph, or make a first-hand inspection from a vantage point of our selected stream or river, is anything that would cause the gold to drop or be deposited. Namely, slower water, the inside bends or sharp turns in the river, wide spots in the river which have a slower flow of water, and obstacles such as large boulders, outcroppings of bedrock, deep pools, fissures, or large cracks in the bedrock, particularly those that run perpendicular to the course of the stream.

Deposits are formed by slackened current downstream from obstacles.

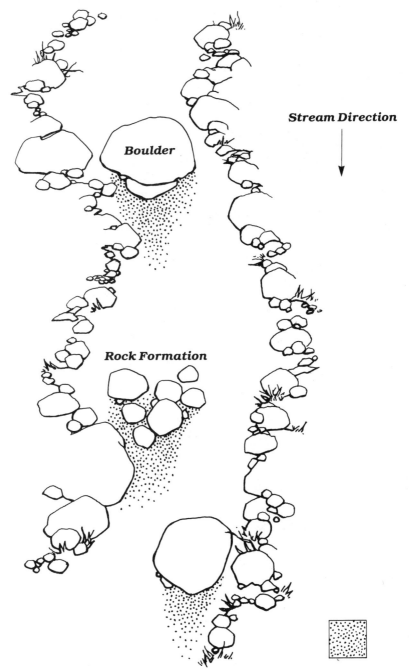

Stream Direction

Boulder

Rock Formation

Area to Prospect

Gold deposited in such locations will remain there until a greater force, i.e., a heavier flood stage with related greater water volume, moves it to a new location. Its resistance will be reinforced by the nature of gold, that is, its density will cause it to settle as deep as it can in the stream bed until it reaches a point of resistance it can not overcome such as bedrock.

The variations on the above set of circumstances are infinite. In the natural state it will be much less common to find only one set of circumstances or obstacles to impede the movement of gold. More than likely there will be several combinations of compound curves, boulders of various sizes, fast and slow water, and several types of sub-surface obstacles to trap our elusive prize.

Rather than list additional simplified examples, your knowledge of the basics will allow you to imagine for yourself the various circumstances that would not allow the gold to escape its transportation through the swift waters of mountain streams.

Learn to *Read* the Stream

It's best if you first study your particular stream selection from both an overview of the area and an on-the-spot inspection at the water level. Walk the stream bed for several hundred yards in either direction. Study the various locations of rocks and boulders. These will range in size from baseballs to basketballs to boulders as big as a house. All have come to rest during past runoffs; like our gold, unwilling passengers riding the force of the flood water. You'll notice that on the inside curves, as we discussed, there will likely be deposits known as "gravel bars." These are excellent sites for the deposit of gold. Look for the perpendicular crevices, particularly if they coincide with the inside curve of the stream or in combination with other obstructions such as bedrock outcroppings. Also, as you make your on-site inspection by walking up and down the stream bank observe not only the present flow of the water, its rapids, and its wide areas, etc., but also consider recent flood waters 5 to 10 feet above normal level, and the less frequent floods – those that occur every 20 to 30 years and which raise the water to a raging river 20 and 25 feet above where you are now standing. There might easily be a large nugget hung up somewhere undiscovered by those looking only at how the river is flowing today.

As mentioned, the various examples I've cited involved the hypothetical situation of introducing our test nugget into the stream to see how it reacts to the flow of water. To better understand where we might find concentrations of gold, which can range in size from almost microscopic grains (flour gold) and matchhead-sized pieces up to and hopefully including nuggets, we will have to bear

Daguerreotype, circa. 1852. Miners working a Long Tom in Auburn Ravine. *(Courtesy of Wells Fargo Bank History Room)*

in mind that the gold we are after did not necessarily erode from the same location or at the same
time. The deposits you will be looking for will be
those which have accumulated over a long period
of time, although, as streams are replenished
annually, a considerable amount of gold will have
arrived more recently.

What we are looking for are those areas
which contain an accumulation of gold, not necessarily overlooked by the original '49ers, but
perhaps a deposit accumulated from the last 100
years and perhaps several major floods. This is not
to say that the original '49ers cleaned out every
area they worked, for their methods of recovery
were sometimes crude and haphazard. It's estimated that over one third of the gold they mined
during the hydraulic operations was lost during
the process as well as a considerable amount lost
through the crudely constructed "long toms" that
ran for miles along the mother lode terrain.

Another method brought into play in the
early mining fields used water in a more aggressive
role. *Hydraulicking* was the practice of directing
high pressure hoses along the canyon walls to
wash down "bench" deposits and other potentially
rich gravels into crudely constructed wooden
sluice boxes or long toms some exceeding one
quarter mile in length. These operations caused
severe silt build up in the streams and eventually
contributed to damaging build ups in the Sacramento River and in the San Francisco Bay.

You can see the results of using these huge
hoses to carve the paydirt today in scarred hillsides that resemble a minor version of the hillsides
of the Grand Canyon. It has also been estimated
by local miners to whom I've talked that 10 to 15
percent of the placer gold found today is gold that
was present and undiscovered during the gold rush
of 1849/50. The reason, as stated earlier, is that

Hydraulic Washing.

The scene above represents a company of miners washing down the hill by
the Hydraulic process. The water from
above being confined in a strong hose,
is played through a pipe upon the bank
of sand and gravel, with great force and
effect. By this process, great quantities of earth are washed down, and
passing through a long sluice, the gold
is there saved. Sometimes where the
gold is very fine, the Guyaskutus is of
great value to the miner, saving nearly
enough to pay his weekly water bill.

when these miners moved into a rich area they would move on to easier pickings when the original area they were working seemed depleted or was located in an area inaccessible to them (stream bottoms that the early argonauts were unable to divert [Flume] thereby laying it open to mine). I've seen several respectable-sized nuggets that were recently taken in the Yuba River from areas very heavily worked by several generations of miners. This is not something you should expect to find on your first, or even second, try at gold mining, but perhaps the next time, or the next time. . . .

Another point we will discuss in more detail when we talk about the techniques of panning — but one which you should be aware of when making your observations — is the presence, in the likely areas of gold deposits, of old square nails,

Miners working a sluice box.
(Courtesy of The California Historical Society, San Francisco)

bits of iron, buckshot, spent bullets, and concentrations of black sand. These elements are proportionally heavier for their size than the rock around them and generally are associated with concentrations of gold. Because of their weight, each settles in areas of lesser resistance, as will our elusive metal.

I strongly suggest spending at least several hours, and ideally several trips, if feasible, during the winter or spring months to observe various areas and subsections during the spring runoff. This is the time to study the flow of the water and to also get a feel for which areas should prove richer than others. When the more temperate weather arrives, you can spend that time recovering gold with a better understanding of where it will most likely be found. On these various shorter excursions you might want to bring along several hand tools to sample each area, thereby eliminating the obviously unprofitable zones. Take notes and pick land marks that you can refer to since an area can look substantially different several months later.

Cross-section of stream bedrock showing cracks, crevices, and depressions that form "pockets" to trap gold.

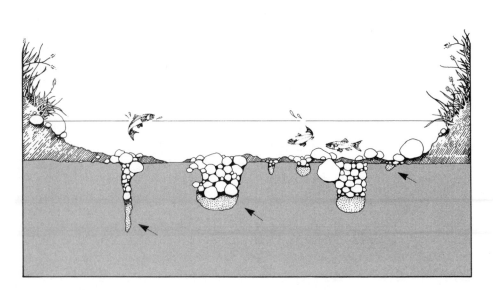

Placer Paydirt

Points to Remember: Look first to the obvious: large cracks, crevices, fissures (particularly those at points where the river or stream will slacken, or wide points, changes in direction, etc.), and the inside bends in the curves of the stream (more than likely associated with deposits of gravel). Observe areas where the river slows down for *any* reason (where the course of the river widens, after a set of rapids, deep pools in the riverbed or where the gradient dissipates thereby slowing flow). Check downstream from intersections of fault lines. Notice sections of river wherever the water current might slacken because of obstructions (boulders, outcroppings of bedrock, etc.). Be on the lookout for concentrations of black sand, old nails, horseshoes, etc. Sample depressions in rocks, particularly those that have many small boulders jammed into the depressions. Check and take a bucket of the material that is caught up in the tangle of exposed tree roots at the water's edge. Make notes of areas in the midsection of the stream where quantities of large boulders have dropped at the point at which the river or stream has widened. Pay attention to any area or condition that would have caused the carrying power of the stream to be reduced. Also look for large boulders that, although "beached" now, were at some time surrounded or completely submerged by a long-forgotten spring flood. Winter or early spring survey trips will reveal mid-stream boulders high and dry and easily accessible by mid-summer. It also pays to check out areas where there's evidence of placer tailings from the "old" days, where miners in the desire to cover as much ground as possible often exhibited "haste made waste" in their recovery methods.

Think about the stream geology we spoke of earlier. Learn to 'read' the stream and the factors that determine the speed and volume of its water. Be on the lookout for areas with black sand along the sandy river banks and areas where the swift water would slacken to allow the heavier gold to settle-out (usually at about a 45 degree angle downstream). Look for areas at the stream bottom where such heavy objects as lost tools, pieces of broken machinery, and other dense objects have come to rest.

In areas containing schistose bedrock, break open the outer slabs with a pry-bar and work out the material contained in the crevices. Check areas where you suspect the original river channel may differ from its present course. Its presence can be detected by the rounded, "river-worn" rocks it contains. Dig beneath the "overburden" wherever possible and attempt to reach bedrock.

Prospecting for Quartz Veins

The following section is reprinted from Special Publications 41, courtesy of the California Division of Mines and Geology.

A gold-bearing vein may or may not be visible on the surface. During its slow process of breaking down, gold becomes scattered in the soil, usually close to or on the bed-rock below the vein. The movement of gold eroded from a vein is like the flow of water.

For example, visualize a small vein of gold-ore occurring on a hillside and running in a direction nearly parallel to the base of the hill. If, at a point about twenty feet below, and on a line parallel to this vein, a number of samples five or ten feet apart are taken by digging down to or nearly to bedrock, they will likely yield gold colors in panning (a color is one visible flake or speck of gold). On a line forty feet below, and parallel to the vein, samples taken in the same manner may also give gold colors, but they will probably be fewer in number to the pan. At sixty, or perhaps as far as two hundred feet below, colors might still be obtained. In searching for gold deposit conditions are reversed: the source is unknown, but the finding of colors is an indication of the existence of a gold-bearing vein at some higher point.

In prospecting a hill, holes are usually dug near its base at intervals of fifty feet or more, and the alluvium near bedrock is panned carefully. When colors are found, the prospector ascends about twenty feet where he digs more holes in a line parallel to the first row. He pans samples on this line and then climbs about twenty feet higher and starts his new line of holes over the point where he obtained his best sample. He is attempting to follow the gold flow to its source by picking up in his pan little specks of the scattered metal. This method of prospecting is called "post-holing" on account of its resemblance to digging such holes to obtain samples.

Prospecting a hillside: Beginning at dot No. 1 a sample was taken, and then again every 50 to 100 feet. At point 8 the best prospect was found. Samples were then taken as represented by + until the crest of the hill was reached; in this case the vein was rich, but did not crop out.

Gold can usually be found on the bedrock of creeks or gullies in gold-bearing regions. To search for gold in a dry creek, find a place in the watercourse where the bedrock is exposed or nearly exposed. Gold lodges under large rocks and in cracks in the solid formation. Find a fracture in the bedrock. Pry it open with a pick or bar. Your pan filled with water should be handy. Lift out the rocks as they are broken, and wash them in the pan, scraping off any adhering clay or sand. Scrape up all the sand from the crevice and place it in the pan. A small paint brush, a spoon and an old table or putty knife are useful in scraping up all the fine sand that might be lodged in a crevice or under a boulder. Scrape the bedrock vigorously and brush up the sand and dust carefully, for the gold flakes sink deeply. Sometimes three or more scrapings from different parts of the creek may be obtained for one panning test. Pan very carefully. If gold is found, ascend the watercourse and continue to pan at spacings of fifty feet or more. When a point is reached where panning does not yield colors, or the amount of colors greatly diminishes, go back to where it was last obtained and "post-hole" on the hillside.

With a pencil and paper one could outline the probable course of quartz or float from a vein and plan the finding of the deposit by tracing the cast-off flakes of gold or pieces of quartz.

Disintegrated quartz that has separated from its vein and become scattered, follows a course like that of the foregoing described gold, only it is likely to travel farther in its downward course. Quartz float can be traced to its source by careful observation.

In testing quartz for gold, pulverize a small amount to the fineness of sand. A small mortar and pestle is necessary for such testing. A large handful of fines will be necessary. Pan very carefully.

Learn to identify quartz. Use a magnetized knifeblade to remove fragments of iron. Have any heavy unknown mineral found in panning identified, but try to learn to identify the nearly black grains of iron oxides. Have quartz that contains fine-grained pyrite or lead minerals assayed for gold.

TOMING.—The above represents three men working with a Tom; two are vigorously picking down and shoveling the dirt into the upper part of the Tom,— and the other is moving it about with a hoe or shovel, to wash it and throw out the larger rocks or riddlings. The gold, dirt and water passes thro' a seive or tom-iron at the lower end into a riffle box underneath, where the gold is saved.

CHAPTER III

Putting Together
Your "Grubstake"...

S ince you will probably be travelling to the
mountains prior to the summer months, at
least for your survey trips, there is a good
chance you will encounter some adverse weather
conditions. It is therefore advisable to carry in
your vehicle equipment suited to the locality, such
as tire chains, poncho or foul weather gear, insect
repellent, and, of course, a good set of boots.

It is usually helpful and a practical safety
consideration not to travel alone. This is particularly true in areas where you may have to hike
several hundred feet or several miles off the main
road in order to reach your chosen location. It is
also advisable, if this is the case, to let someone
know approximately where you are going and your
expected time of return in the event you don't
arrive within a reasonable period of time. If you are
hiking in, along with your prospecting tools it is
generally a good idea to carry a small pouch or kit
containing some basic survival items such as a
compass, salt tablets, first aid kit, and signal
mirror, along with a canteen and perhaps something to eat. All these items can be put into a small
backpack or "fanny pack" like those worn around
the waist by the ski patrol.

Another point worth mentioning: if you plan
to hike down a canyon to either reconnoiter, pan,
or even fish, allow yourself enough time to climb

out in the daylight. More so in winter, but also in summer months, the light fades very quickly when it approaches sunset. At the end of a long day fatigue can slow you down and make you careless.

This past summer, while camping in the early evening at the top of our claim, we were summoned by a very exhausted and shook-up fisherman. It seems he and a partner had fished too long, misjudged the time, and lost the trail they took down the ravine. The younger man had managed to 'muscle' his way up the side but his partner was stuck on a very sharp, loose wall and caught quite literally between a rock and a hard place. Fortunately, I had a 100-foot section of rope which we were able to anchor to a large fir, lower to the man and pull him up from the tight spot, creel of rainbow trout and all. Starting a half-hour earlier would have prevented the potential tragedy since they had missed the entrance to the trail by less than 100 feet!

Be aware of prevailing weather conditions!
(Courtesy of The California Historical Society, San Francisco)

Prospecting Gear

    A good set of shoes will make the experience safer and more comfortable. If you are operating along a stream bed in the summertime an old pair of sneakers make negotiating the stream safer and easier on the feet. In addition, I've listed below several "sampling" basics:

Gold Pan	Pry Bar
Shovel, Hand-pick, Crevice Tool	Whistbroom
	Old Spoon
Bucket	Several vials to store gold
Coffee can or similar-sized container	Tweezers
	Magnet
Garden Trowel	Small magnifying glass

    Prospecting is, by definition, the testing for values in each area of your search for the most likely spot to find gold. The gold pan, a pick, and small shovel are the tools most used for this stage of recreational mining. The gold pan is also a

Early Western scene. *(Photo courtesy of the Donald Simon Collection)*

valuable "sampling" tool that can ultimately lead you to the source of the colors.

The gold pan can either be steel or the plastic variety. Each has its advantages. The traditionalists prefer the metal pan. They claim it is more durable and can be used for other purposes such as a fry pan or wash bowl. The standard size is 16 inches; however, the 12-inch and 14-inch models are easier to handle in the beginning and are fine for sampling an area.

I prefer the new high-impact, plastic variety since it is lighter in weight, certainly as durable under normal use, and can be bought in either black or green to contrast the gold against a dark background. Additionally, the many plastic pans available have "traps" or cheater riffles moulded into them to aid the novice in the recovery of fine gold. Pan selection is a matter of personal preference, but if you're hiking back for any distance you might prefer the advantage of the lesser

Gear–Gear: the basic tools of the prospector.

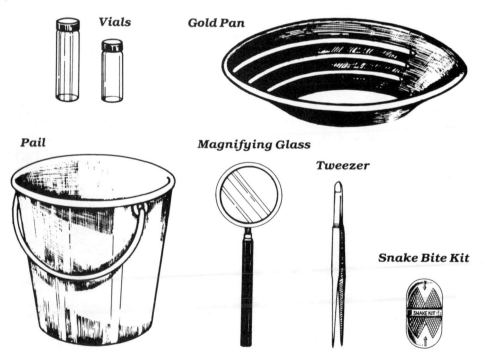

Vials   Gold Pan

Pail   Magnifying Glass

Tweezer

Snake Bite Kit

weight of the plastic pan so that you can carry additional equipment of your choice.

If you should choose the metal pan, it is necessary before its initial use to burn or "blue" it. The purpose is to both burn off any oils used in its manufacture as well as darken the surface appearance so that the gold can be seen more easily. The easiest way to burn off the pan is to put it on a stove for several minutes or right into an open fire.

Each type of pan comes in various sizes from 6 to 18 inches; 8 to 12 inches is generally the most popular. An additional advantage of the plastic pan is that if you plan to do any electronic prospecting with the aid of a metal detector, any material added to a plastic pan can be easily checked by passing the detector head over it. Additionally, concentrations of black sands, when dry, can be separated from the gold dust by moving a magnet in a circular motion under the pan.

Shovel

Pry Bar

Rock Hammer

Crevice Tool

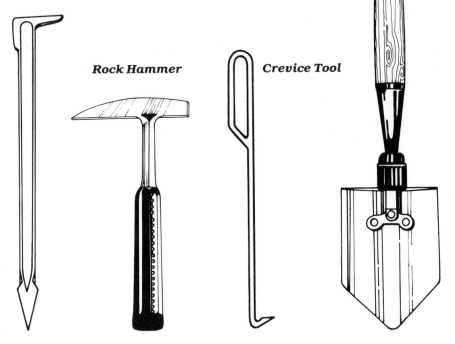

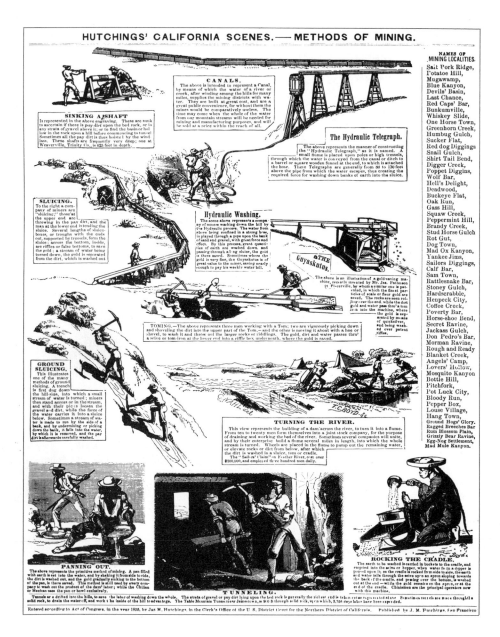

NAMES OF MINING LOCALITIES.

Salt Pork Ridge,
Potatoe Hill,
Mugawamp,
Blue Kanyon,
Devils' Basin,
Last Chance,
Red Caps' Bar,
Bunkumville,
Whiskey Slide,
One Horse Town,
Greenhorn Creek,
Humbug Gulch,
Sucker Flat,
Red dog Diggings
Snail Gulch,
Shirt Tail Bend,
Digger Creek,
Poppet Diggins,
Wolf Bar,
Hell's Delight,
Deadwood,
Buckeye Flat,
Oak Run,
Gass Hill,
Squaw Creek,
Peppermint Hill,
Brandy Creek,
Stud Horse Gulch
Rot Gut,
Dog Town,
Mad Ox Kanyon,
Yankee Jims,
Sailors Diggings,
Calf Bar,
Sam Town,
Rattlesnake Bar,
Stoney Gulch,
Hardscrabble,
Henpeck City,
Coffee Creek,
Poverty Bar,
Horse-shoe Bend,
Secret Ravine,
Jackass Gulch,
Don Pedro's Bar,
Morman Ravine,
Rough and Ready
Blanket Creek,
Angels' Camp,
Lovers' Hollow,
Mosquito Kanyon
Bottle Hill,
Pitchfork,
Pot Luck City,
Bloody Run,
Pepper Box,
Louse Village,
Hang Town,
Ground Hogs' Glory.
Ragged Breeches Bar
Rum Blossom Plain,
Grizzly Bear Ravine,
Egg-Nog Settlement,
Mad Mule Kanyon.

SINKING A SHAFT

Is represented in the above engraving. These are sunk to ascertain if there is pay dirt upon the bed rock, or in any strata of gravel above it; or to find the basin or hol low in the rock upon a hill before commencing to tunnel. Sometimes all the pay dirt is thus hoist t by the wind lass. These shafts are frequently very deep; one at Weaverville, Trinity Co., is 625 feet in depth.

CANALS.

The above is intended to represent a Canal, by means of which the water of a river or creek, after winding among the hills for many miles, supplies the mining districts with water. They are built at great cost, and are a great public convenience, for without them the mines would be comparatively useless. The time may come when the whole of the water from our mountain streams will be needed for mining and manufacturing purposes, and will be sold at a price within the reach of all.

The Hydraulic Telegraph.

The above represents the manner of constructing the "Hydraulic Telegraph," as it is named. A small flume is placed upon poles or high tressels, through which the water is conveyed from the canal or ditch to a barrel or square wooden funnel at the end, to which is attached the hose. These Telegraphs are generally from 80 to 130 feet above the pipe from which the water escapes, thus creating the required force for washing down banks of earth into the sluice.

SLUICING.

To the right a company of miners are "sluicing;" those at the upper end are throwing in the pay dirt, and the man at the lower end is tending the sluice. Several lengths of sluice-boxes, or troughs with the ends out, supported by tressels, form the sluice; across the bottom, inside, are riffles or false bottoms, to save the gold; a stream of water being turned down, the gold is separated from the dirt, which is washed out

Hydraulic Washing.

The scene above represents a company of miners washing down the hill by the Hydraulic process. The water from above being confined in a strong hose, is played through a pipe upon the bank of sand and gravel, with great force and effect. By this process, great quantities of earth are washed down, and passing through a l ng sluice, the gold is there saved. Sometimes where the gold is very fine, the Guyaskutas is of great value to the miner, saving nearly enough to pay his weekly water bill.

THE Guyaskutus.

The above is an illustration of a gold-saving machine, recently invented by Mr. Jas. Patterson of Placerville, by whom a similar one is patented, in which the finest particles of scale or flour gold are saved. The rocks are seen rolling over the end, while the dirt gold and water pass thro' a tom iron into the machine, where the gold is separated by means of quicksilver, and being washed over patent riffles.

TOMING.

TOMING.—The above represents three men working with a Tom; two are vigorously picking down and shoveling the dirt into the upper part of the Tom,— and the other is moving it about with a hoe or shovel, to wash it and throw out the larger rocks or riddlings. The gold, dirt and water passes thro' a seive or tom-iron at the lower end into a riffle box underneath, where the gold is saved.

GROUND SLUICING.

This illustrates one of the many methods of ground sluicing. A trench is first dug down the hill-side, into which a small stream of water is turned; miners then stand across or in the stream, and with their pic s loosen the gravel and dirt, while the force of the water carries it into a sluice below. Sometimes a stream of water is made to run by the side of a bank, and by undermining or guiding down the bank, it falls into the water, by which it is removed, and the pay dirt is afterwards carefully washed.

TURNING THE RIVER.

This view represents the building of a dam across the river, to turn it into a flume. From ten to twenty men form themselves into a joint stock company, for the purpose of draining and working the bed of the river. Sometimes several companies will unite, and by their enterprise build a flume several miles in length, into which the whole stream is turned. Wheels are placed in the flume to pump out the remaining water, or elevate rocks or dirt from below, after which the dirt is washed in a sluice, tom or cradle. The "Sail rs' Claim" on Feather River, cost over $900,000, and employed three hundred men daily.

PANNING OUT.

The above represents the primitive method of mining. A pan fill-d with earth is set into the water, and by shaking it from side to side, the dirt is washed out, and the gold gradually sinking to the bottom of the pan, is there saved. This method is still used by every company to wash out the product of the days' labor; while the Chilian or Mexican uses the pan or bowl exclusively.

TUNNELING.

Tunnels are d ifted into the hills, to save the labor of washing down the whole. The strata of gravel or pay dirt lying upon the bed rock is generally the richest and is taken cut as represented above. Sometimes tunnels are made through solid rock, to drain the water off, and work t he inside of the hill to advant ge. The Table Mountain Tunnel near Jamestown, is 900 ft through solid rock, upon which, 3,786 days labor have been expended.

ROCKING THE CRADLE.

The earth to be washed is carried in buckets to the cradle, and emptied into the seive or hopper, when water from a dipper is poured upon it; as the cradle is rocked from side to side, the earth and water falls through the seive upon an apron sloping towards the back of the cradle, and passing over the bottom, is washed out at the end—while the gold remains on the apron, or at the end of the cradle. Chinamen are the principal operators now with this machine.

Entered according to Act of Congress, in the year 1855, by Jas M. Hutchings, in the Clerk's Office of the U. S. District Court for the Northern District of California.   Published by J. M. Hutchings, San Francisco

Hutchings' Mining Methods (*Courtesy of the California Historical Society*)

CHAPTER IV

Methods: Then & Now

We'll begin this section with an overview of the different methods commonly used to recover placer gold. Each of these and their variations were used in the major "rushes" and are depicted in the various illustrations that accompany the text. Where larger companies or groups of men were available, additional techniques were employed to divert the natural flow of the streams or to make use of its power in operating some of the equipment. If water was scarce, canals or flumes were built – in some areas up to several miles long – to bring water to the paydirt.

We'll confine ourselves for the most part to that equipment and manner which you're likely to use or see in operation by weekend miners. Tunneling techniques, stamp-mills, and the like can be pursued at another time.

There are several methods for the recovery of gold, each depending on how deeply committed you want to get and the amount of time and money you wish to invest. The simplest, least expensive, and primary method is *panning*. The object of panning is to separate and concentrate the heavier material by washing away the lighter. The most common panning method is called "wet" panning, in which case a ready supply of water must be available in sufficient quantity. This is generally done at the stream bank.

Panning can also be used as a means to an

end, that is, for sampling a likely area where a more extensive operation will later take place. A pan full of potentially auriferous material can be checked from several different areas along the contour of the stream. More than likely, a spot that shows 'color' at the shallower depths will be richer as you dig deeper to where the gold has settled. This, however, will not always be true. Rich ground will be laid down by the erosion process in layers depending on the conditions that prevailed and in 'stringers' along with the black 'sands'. The idea is to survey and sample likely areas with the pan before settling in for the day or bringing in your heavier tools (pick axe, crow/pry bar, sluice box, etc.).

Since pannng ultimately brings us to the essence of what we're after, I feel it should be described in detail. Unfortunately, as a picture is to a thousand words, so is a demonstration of immeasurable value. Study the text, watch an

Six miners with rocker. Note one miner showing nugget in pan. *(Daguerreotype courtesy of The Bancroft Library,)*

"old-timer" if you can, and practice. You'll catch on in no time. Speed isn't the motive, efficiency is.

How to Pan

Select, through the various observations we have discussed, the most likely areas for an accumulation of gold. Keep in mind that the water action and settlement of the gravel will cause the gold to sink as deep as it can, stopping only upon reaching either bedrock or dense clay. Therefore, when at all possible, dig down to the bedrock and clean out each crack *thoroughly* with the aid of a screw driver or crevice tool. Pry these cracks open and sweep them clean with a small brush or whisk broom. Depressions and holes in the bedrock, which contain stones and rocks jammed into place and held by sand and gravel, should also be pried loose and the material panned. Shake or wash all roots and compacted twigs thoroughly into the pan. Next, with your pan no more than three-quarters full:

1. Settle yourself into a slow-moving section of the stream bed where you can squat and work the

pan in the water. Waders or waterproof boots will insulate your feet from the cold stream. Place the pan completely under the surface of the water by several inches. With one hand, thoroughly mix and knead the material with the water to completely saturate everything in the pan. Be sure to break up all clogs of dirt, especially any clay-like soils. Wash and break up all root material.

2. Next, with the pan still under the water's surface, begin to vigorously shake the pan back and forth and from side to side keeping the contents within the pan. This action will settle the gold and cause the lighter material and muddied water to rise to the surface and be carried off in the stream current. Make sure the water in which you're working is not moving too fast since it would be difficult to regulate the amount of unwanted material washing out of the pan. If you are using a plastic pan with traps or riffles, these should be positioned at 12 o'clock.

PANNING OUT.

The above represents the primitive method of mining. A pan filled with earth is set into the water, and by shaking it from side to side, the dirt is washed out, and the gold gradually sinking to the bottom of the pan, is there saved. This method is still used by every company to wash out the product of the days' labor; while the Chilian or Mexican uses the pan or bowl exclusively.

3. The *thoroughly washed* larger rocks can now be removed. Continue shaking the pan to settle the gold.

The "Tennessee Partner" *(Courtesy Levi Strauss & Co.)*

4. With the pan still submerged and the edge furthest away from you tipped slightly downward, begin a circular or swirling motion either clockwise or counter-clockwise. The material in the pan should be in a state of liquid suspension. This will "float" the lighter material to the top where it will be carried out of the pan. You may rake some of the top-most material off at this point since the gold will have settled close to the pan's bottom. Once again, place the pan under the water and "resettle" the gold by shaking the pan.

5. Continue washing and floating the lighter (blond) sands and other material out of the top of the pan. This action duplicates the action of the stream, 'settling' the gold into the bottom of the pan. Stubborn pebbles should be picked out by hand.

6. Continue the circular motion. Each slight 'thrust' eliminates more material. Proceed

slowly until your proficiency has increased. Stop periodically to resettle the gold in the crease of the pan by rapping the pan's rim two or three times with the palm of your hand. The "traps" or riffles formed in the side of the pan help hold the fine gold.

7. After several minutes you will have only the heavier material remaining in the bottom of the pan. This will usually be the "black sand," a combination of magnetic and nonmagnetic irons and pyrites. Continue to slowly wash this 'concentrate,' being very careful that the fine gold doesn't work its way up the rim. Resettle as necessary. An alternative method to panning down this concentrate is to hold the pan with either one or both hands with its lower edge at a 20–30 degree downward angle, and slowly dip a third or so of the black sand in and out of the water to further reduce the concentrate. Watch for any signs of gold working its way up the rim.

8. When you've worked the black sand concentrate down to the point that only a tablespoon or two remains, remove the pan from the water. Put *just enough* water in the pan to permit the concentrate to swirl. Now, with the pan out of the water and level, start the water moving in a circular motion, spreading the concentrate into a thin layer across the surface of the bottom of the pan and exposing the 'colors!' These flakes can be removed with the aid of a tweezers or with the tip of your finger moistened with saliva. Place the gold into one of the various glass vials that are sold in most hardware and hobby shops. Some miners prefer to fill these small vials with water to help the gold "drop" into the bottle. Excessive black sand that may end up in the vial can be removed by passing a small

magnet along the outside of the vial working the sand up to its opening.

An alternate method entails drying out the concentrate in the sun, then passing a magnet under your *plastic* pan to separate the sand from the gold. If you find buckshot, remnants of square nails, or slivers of lead, the odds are in your favor that you have found a good spot since these heavier items are often associated with concentrations of fine gold. Keep removing and sampling deeper material. Gold is extremely heavy and will settle deeper than other items of similar size.

Don't be in a hurry, especially when you're first learning. It takes at least ten minutes to satis-factorily settle-out a large pan of gravel. If you are doing your clean-up of *concentrate* from a sluice, rocker, or dredge, you'll need to spend even more time. This is the heaviest, richest material, there-fore don't risk losing several hours work by saving five minutes with the pan.

Panning is basically a simple procedure, but one with many individual styles. It's best to practice before your initial trip by placing a few BBs or fine buckshot into some test material and pan this in a large wash tub at home. If you can

Early print showing various contemporary mining methods. *(Courtesy of the Dale Chappell Collection)*

find all of the 'simulated' nuggets in the remaining concentrate, you will have achieved enough proficiency to feel confident that you won't lose the heavier gold.

While knowing how to pan is basic and necessary for almost all other phases of prospecting, it is not generally used to recover significant amounts of the metal. There are easier and more efficient methods of doing so.

Gold Pan Sieve

The *Sieve* is a very useful device for increasing productivity while panning. Most of those I've seen and used are made of light-weight, high impact plastic and, depending on the size of the gold pan, will fit inside or over it.

In use, gravel is shoveled into the sieve and pan combination. Both are held together, placed in the stream, and shaken back and forth for a minute or so to "sift" the gravel. This allows the finer material to pass through the mesh (usually three-eighths inches) and into the pan. The sieve is then checked for nuggets and the debris is discarded. This action classifies the gravel, eliminates the need to pick out the stones one at a time, and cuts panning in half. The material remaining in the pan is then washed in the usual manner.

In *all of* the techniques employed to mine gold, *the amount of the metal recovered is directly proportional to the volume of material processed.* In the case of panning, which is relatively slow, the sieve enables the user to process considerably more gravel in less time and with less effort. The sieve or a coarse screen can also be adapted to sort material prior to its introduction in the hopper end of a sluice or rocker-box.

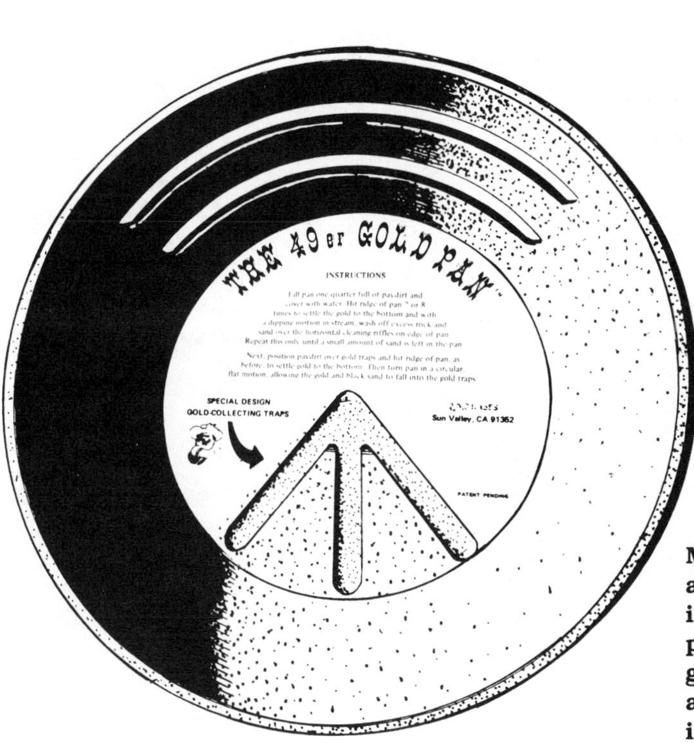
THE 49er GOLD PAN
INSTRUCTIONS
Fill pan one quarter full of paydirt and cover with water. Hit ridge of pan 7 or 8 times to settle the gold to the bottom and with a dipping motion in stream, wash off excess rock and sand over the horizontal cleaning riffles on edge of pan. Repeat this only until a small amount of sand is left in the pan.
Next, position paydirt over gold traps and hit ridge of pan, as before, to settle gold to the bottom. Then turn pan in a circular, flat motion, allowing the gold and black sand to fall into the gold traps.
SPECIAL DESIGN GOLD-COLLECTING TRAPS
Sun Valley, CA 91352
PATENT PENDING

Modern gold pans are made of high impact black plastic that show gold at a glance and contain built-in riffles and gold trap. ***(Courtesy of 49er Products)***

The Sniffer

A device sometimes called a gold sniffer or suction gun can be helpful when attempting to clean out a pocket mixed with water and gravel. The nose of the device is placed into the loosened material in the crevice and the plunger withdrawn, creating a suction which fills the canister with water, sand, and gold (see illustration).

Take the material you plan to process from as close to the bedrock as you can dig. The bedrock poses an impermeable layer through which the gold cannot settle. Pockets, cracks and crevices should be *thoroughly* cleaned out. These are natural gold traps. The more compacted the stones and gravel, the greater the likelihood of holding the eroded metal.

The canister contents are then panned.

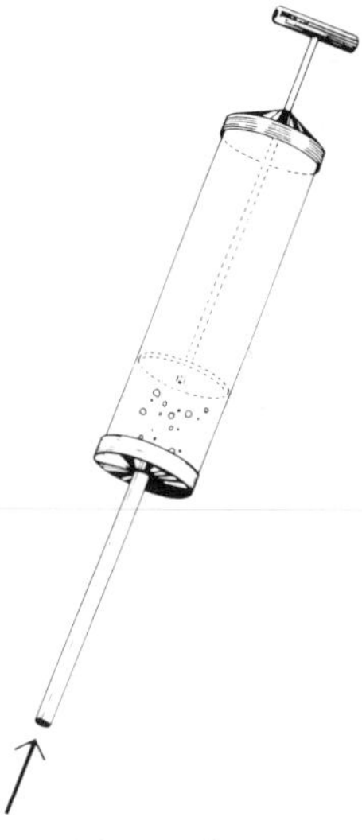

Gold suction gun or "sniffer." Sucks up water, sand and gold.

Dry Placer Operations

Drywashing, or dry panning as it is sometimes called, is done as the name implies in an area
where no water is available at the time. It can be
either desert or an area having seasonal runoff.
The locations for the latter are generally in dry
placer areas of desert stream beds. These streams
are rarely dry year-round and the formations to
look for here are the same as for active streams.
Here again, gravity is the main force for separating
the gold from the other materials. There has been a
considerable amount of gold recovered in the
desert areas but it rarely received the publicity or
the glamour of the mountain mines.

Winnowing is the fundamental dry-wash
method. It involves screening out all the coarse
gravel, then placing the 'fines' in a blanket and
tossing them into a good breeze, one man at each
end of the blanket. The lighter particles are blown
away by the wind, while the heavier particles fall
back onto the blanket. The weave of the blanket

Winnowing.
*(Courtesy, California
Division of Mines
and Geology)*

tends to catch and hold onto fine gold.

A *dry washer* is a device that uses a trough similar to a sluice box in construction. The riffles area of the dry washer is placed in an upright position at a sharp angle perpendicular to the trough. The dry gravel and sand is on a slight downward slope. A shaking, vibrating action by means of a mechanical, manual or motor-driven crank causes the material to feed over the riffles, settling the heavier gold to the bottom of the trough. It is essential in both winnowing and dry washing that the material be thoroughly dry and disintegrated, having first separated or pulverized the coarser material. Damp gravel obtained below the surface material should be dry throughout to maximize the recovery process. There are a number of dry washer designs available from mining supply houses or one can be built in the home workshop.

The traditional method of panning can be

A "crevice tool" or long screwdriver is used to thoroughly clean out cracks and fissures. Pan the accumulated material.

67

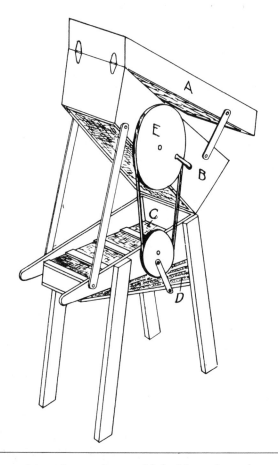

used by taking along a large old-fashioned wash bucket and a couple of five gallon cans of water and working the pan in a large bucket of water.

    It should be noted for those not familiar with desert areas that temperatures, depending on altitude, can be severe with little natural cover to shield or hold the heat. Daytime summer heat can be deadly, as well as the exposure to cold winter nights. Perhaps even more than in other places, the necessity of leaving word with a friend on where you plan to go and when you expect to return is important since it takes considerably less time for a situation to turn critical. Proper clothing, including a hat to shield you from the sun's heat

Dry Washer.
(Courtesy, California Division of Mines and Geology)

and glare, a small survival pouch (see details, page 95), and an adequate supply of drinking water are all essential.

Operation of a Sluice

Today many prospectors make use of an abbreviated version of the '49ers 'sluice-box'. Its use is called *sluicing*. It is a relatively short trough with a flat, smooth forward end and a riffle section. The sluice generally is placed right in the stream itself and works on the same principle as the flow of water along the bottom of the stream bed. A sluice can easily be made with basic tools from your workshop and several sections can be made for easy transportation. Several sizes are available in

Two miners operating a modern sluice box. Note the sieve used to sort the larger rocks.

69

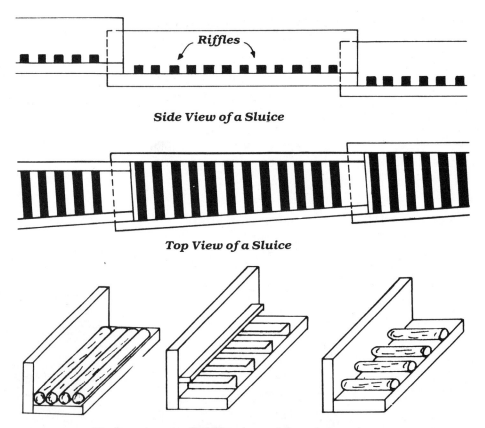

Side View of a Sluice

Top View of a Sluice

Various types of Riffles (one side cut away)

lightweight aluminum from various prospector supply houses. Generally a man can successfully pan anywhere from one-half to one yard of gravel per day. However, using a sluice one person can process six to eight times more material than by panning. It's a miniature 'stream' for purposes of separating the gold from the other river debris.

Sluices are generally four to six feet in length, six to twelve inches wide, with sides six inches high. Like the Long Tom, it is a three-sided, open-ended trough, fitted with a series of perpendicular riffles, cleats or obstructions every few inches which are set on a piece of burlap or indoor-outdoor carpeting.

In order to operate a sluice, place it in a rela-

(Drawing courtesy of California Department of Mines and Geology)

tively fast-moving current close to the bank where you will be working. Tip its head slightly higher than the tail so that the excess material will exit and disperse into the stream. If there is insufficient water running through the sluice, a wingdam made of a dozen or so good-sized rocks (see illustration) can be arranged at its head to divert additional water into the sluice. Generally a long, heavy rock is placed on top so that its weight will hold the sluice securely in place. Rocks can also be used under the head or tail of the box to regulate its pitch and the volume of water necessary to separate and classify the dirt fed into the hopper-end.

Set the sluice-box into the stream so that the water is running through it at a rate fast enough to carry most of the material the full length of the box. Take a pail full of material from a test area (upper end of a gravel bar, lee side of an obstacle, etc.) and begin to slowly pour handfuls of that material into the upper end of the sluice, breaking up the material with your hands to loosen and separate any clay, roots, etc., and sorting out any

Hopper end of sluice box is fed auriferous material for classification. (Inset: Eddy currents are formed behind riffles to trap gold.)

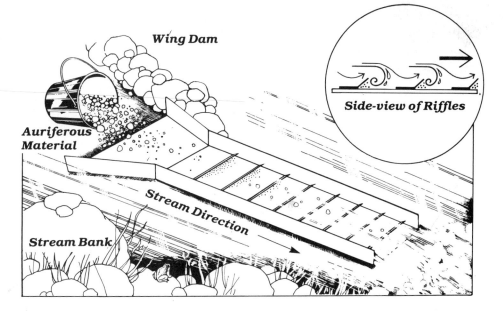

Wing Dam

Side-view of Riffles

Auriferous Material

Stream Direction

Stream Bank

large rocks. Regulate the water passing through the sluice so that enough water keeps the riffles from becoming clogged.

After a while, a build-up of the heavier material and black sand will begin accumulating on the downstream side of the riffles. Regulate the angle of the sluice to pass all or most of the coarser material, letting the black sand (iron pyrites) gather behind the riffles. A few BBs can be dropped in the head to test the water action and obtain the optimum angle. These should ideally end up in the first two or three riffles, as will most of your gold. If they pass much beyond the third or fourth riffle either the water flow through the sluice is too swift or the angle too sharp, and much of your fine gold will be lost. Be sure you break up the clay, if any, since it has a strong tendency to hold on to any fine gold.

The black sand and any gold that will start to build up behind the riffles is doing so because of eddy (contrary) current that is formed behind the man-made riffle or cleat (obstacle). Continue to slowly put in and thoroughly mix the material at the head of the sluice until the riffles are full of 'concentrate.' When this happens (anywhere from two to three buckets of material to a dozen depending on the amount of iron pyrites in the soil), you're ready to 'clean up' and pan down the concentrate to remove the gold.

The purpose of the sluice box is to allow you to remove a much greater amount of 'overburden,' with the aid of the stream, than you would by panning. It's generally wise to sort out larger rocks by hand or through a coarse screen prior to putting the material into the head of the sluice. This practice helps you avoid putting your hands into the area of the sluice to clear these, an action which can sometimes momentarily disrupt the eddy current and wash away the finer gold.

You can also improve the operation by fitting the sluice with a primary section constructed to fit in the 'mouth' of the sluice. This is called a "puddling box" and can be fabricated and fitted to the forward section of either a sluice or Long Tom. It's useful when muddy or clayey material is encountered. It allows this material, which is a notorious 'gold-robber,' to be thoroughly saturated, loosened, and broken prior to passing into the main sluice section.

Clean-up

In order to 'clean up,' stop the flow of water entering the sluice, and carefully remove it to the nearby bank. Remove the riffles, screen, and carpet and wash the concentrate with a bucket of water poured slowly into either a second bucket or your gold pan. *Thoroughly* wash the burlap or carpeting into the bucket until all gold particles are freed.

SLUICING.
To the right a company of miners are "sluicing;" those 'at the upper end are throwing in the pay dirt, and the man at the lower end is tending the sluice. Several lengths of sluice-boxes, or troughs with the ends out, supported by tressels, form the sluice; across the bottom, inside, are riffles or false bottoms, to save the gold; a stream of water being turned down, the gold is separated from the dirt, which is washed out

Your concentrate will be a considerably larger quantity than you would normally find after working down a single pan by the traditional method. The reason is that you have processed several times the amount of material with the sluice box and consequently have a proportionally larger amount of concentrate.

Pan down this concentrate as you normally would, taking each phase slowly. You're working with the heaviest material normally found after the first few steps in an initial panning operation.

When constructing a sluice box, or in an effort to 'improve' the commercially available type, some people replace the carpet material and fit the bottom with a piece of artificial grass or turf which is thought to trap more fine gold. After a season of use, the lining in the sluice bottom (carpet, burlap, turf) can be burned in a large steel gold pan and panned to recover the accumulated fine gold dust.

Rocker Box

An alternative method to sluicing is by the fabrication of a *rocker-box* or *cradle*. The general dimensions of a rocker-box are similar, although each miner in the old days had his own variation. This method was used in the early mining operations in Georgia and the Carolinas. The function of this method is similar to that of the sluice with its own distinct advantage: it uses much less water than either a Long Tom or sluice.

Generally, for ease of operation, two or three people worked in a team. The device resembles an infant's cradle, as its name implies. It consists of a sluice-type open trough with riffles or cleats fashioned along the bottom which has a gradual sloping downward angle. It sits on a set of "rockers" fore and aft and at right angles to its

Cradle rocking on the Stanislaus. "A Book For Travellers and Settlers" by Charles Nordhoff, 1873.
(Courtesy of The California Historical Society, San Francisco)

74

length. At the forward end a box is attached with a coarse screen or sieve to separate the larger rocks, below it an "apron" of carpet is placed at a 30–40 degree angle.

The raw material is fed in the top over the screen which separates the various materials. Water via a bucket, diverted stream flow, or pump, pours into the top thereby pushing the material through the screen where it hits the apron secured beneath and then down to an arrangement similar to a short sluice box. The flow of water, mud, smaller rock and gravel-like material will then pass over the riffles. One man may be digging, a second rapidly pours water over the dirt in the box section and one of the two, or a third partner, 'rocks' the cradle with a jerky motion.

The separation or classification will settle out the gold as in the sluice operation. Again, as the riffles become full, the concentrate is taken out and panned to recover the gold.

The rocker which hasn't been widely used in recent years is experiencing a comeback. Its traditional styling, functional design, and its particular advantages are becoming more widely known. The average miner can pan up to a half cubic yard per day while a rocker operator can process four to five yards per day with less strenuous work. A rocker-box is portable, relatively lightweight and a very efficient hand-operated machine. Since it uses very little water it can be operated in semi-arid areas and even in desert areas with a recirculating water supply.

Long Tom

If conditions warranted its use in the old days a *Long Tom* was employed. It required a steady supply of water and usually two or three men to work it. A Long Tom was a three-sided inclined

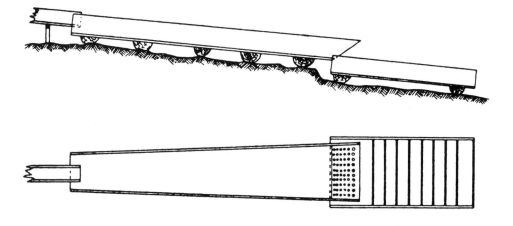

trough that consisted of two sections. The upper end was approximately 10–12 feet long, built wider at the top than the bottom. The lower half of this first section was made of perforated sheet iron that acted as a sieve. The second section, called a riffle-box section, was usually half the length of the sluice and contained cleats or riffles across its bottom. In operation, material was shoveled into the top section of the trough and flushed down its length by a continuous flow of water directed into it. The sieve strained the coarser material while permitting the finer material and gold to pass through into the riffle-box where it became trapped.

    Even this method had its limitation in terms of efficiency and an ingenious 19th century miner decided to modify it further. So was born the *Under Current Sluice*. A wide flat second sluice was placed under the regular sluice. It received its feed from a grating or screen placed in the bottom of the upper sluice and drew off the finer gold so it could be treated in a quieter current, with the larger coarse material and more turbulent water passing overhead.

Diagram of a Long Tom.
(Courtesy, California Division of Mines and Geology)

Hydraulic Concentrator

One of the most novel devices I've used is a combination of the best features of a rocker, Long Tom, and sluice-box. It also doubles as a dredge! The unit is constructed of lightweight aluminum and is powered by a small, powerful two-cycle engine combined with a centrifugal pump. It can be used either to process material located at a distance from flowing water or, in its alternate arrangement, the nozzle/hose assembly is used to suck up gravel from the stream bed.

In an operation conducted away from an immediate supply of water, the engine/pump is placed at a convenient water source to draw water into the pump and deliver it through a long dis-

Hydraulic Concentrator. As illustrated, unit is set up to operate as a suction dredge. *(Courtesy, Keene Engineering Co.)*

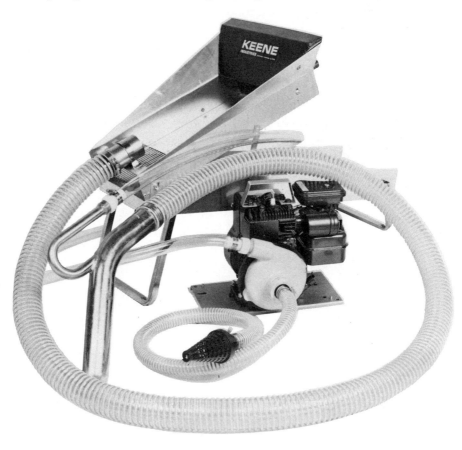

charge hose to the classifier/concentrator unit which is located at the area you are working. Gravel is shoveled into the upper end (hopper) of the concentrator unit, and water from the discharge hose washes the material. It then passes through the grizzly bars to separate the larger rocks and is classified in the lower (riffle) section.

As a dredge, the unit is set up at the stream bank. A suction hose and pressure hose combination are substituted for the discharge hose. The water passing from the water pump through the pressure at the nozzle causes a vacuum in the suction hose which is then used to suck up the potential ore-bearing gravel. This material again flows into the hopper, through the grizzly bars and then is 'sorted' in the riffle section. The gold is trapped in the same manner as in the other devices described earlier. Breakdown of the riffle section, underlying carpet, and cleanup is basically the same as for a rocker or sluice-box.

This unit which is capable of processing a considerable amount of material offers the operator the flexibility of owning one piece of equipment that is suited for both bench and placer operations.

Small, relatively lightweight, modern "back-pack" dredges offer a high degree of portability for getting into rich, virgin areas.

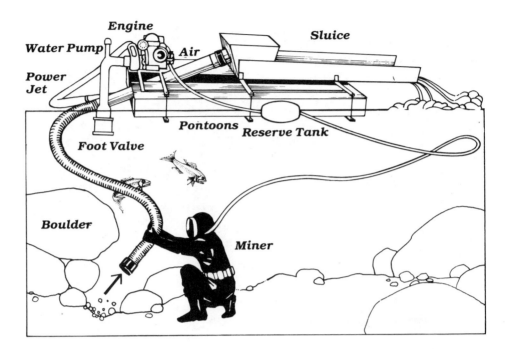

Engine

Water Pump

Air

Power Jet

Sluice

Foot Valve

Pontoons   Reserve Tank

Boulder

Miner

Dredges

The most recent 20th century recreational method for the retrieval of stream placer gold is *dredging*. This method consists of a mechanical pump operated by a gas-powered engine that creates a vacuum. The whole apparatus is floated upon either a pair of large truck inner tubes or a set of pontoons. The vacuum hose is directed to suck up material from the stream bottom and the mixture of water, rock, sand, gravel and gold runs through a sluice where the gold is separated by the riffles.

These dredges generally operate with a several horsepower motor and come in a wide variety of styles and sizes moving quantities, at optimum, which range from one to thirty yards of gravel per hour, depending upon the horse power, hose diameter, altitude, and design of the dredge. The advantages are obvious, and although it would seem at first to be considerably less work than the pick, shovel, and pan method, there is a substantially larger investment in equipment, and

Typical setup of a recreational dredge showing miner directing suction hose.

Author descending with dredge suction hose.

many obstructions that are larger than the capacity of the suction nozzle opening must still be moved manually.

There are several brands of 'portable' or 'backpack' dredges on the market that can be useful in sampling areas prior to committing to heavier equipment. They generally have an intake hose size of 1½ to 2½ inches, and the individual components can be broken down into a package carried by one man. Sufficient capacity for a *full-time* operation generally can't be generated until you trade up to a 3–5-inch model, thereby operating at a rated volume of 8–16 yards per hour of 'classified' material under ideal conditions.

The medium size dredges (3–5 inches) are the most popular because they are relatively lightweight and of moderate cost. Plan to buy or order one in the 'off season' as suppliers have recently not been able to keep up with demand as the price of gold climbs and popularity of the hobby increases.

Depending on the dredge's size, the operator's preference, and other variables (local restrictions, time of year, weather conditions), the operator can stand in the water or use a mask and snorkel while directing the suction hose. Deeper water operations require the use of air and com-pressor units are employed as a supplement to the power equipment. Air lines are used in lieu of scuba tanks for ease of movement, duration, and logistics of resupply. The latter method involves an additional investment in equipment for air com-pressors, reserve tank, hoses, harness, regulators, wet suits, etc., to operate under the surface of the water for several hours at a time. Those afflicted with the more advanced symptoms of 'gold fever' will eventually, and possibly quite rapidly, trade up to this method of pursuing their hobby since the rewards are proportional to the effort.

In principle, the basic elements for selecting a site are the same; that is, deciding on the optimum location where gold would "logically" have settled and drawing as much material, as is feasible in a given period of time, up the suction

Nose of suction hose sucks up gold-bearing gravels at stream bottom.

tube, through the baffle screen and over the riffles to classify and separate the gold from the other river material. There are several detailed books on dredging for gold should this method be of interest.

Large dredges like the one pictured were used to mine vast quantities of low-grade river placer deposits. (Courtesy of Old Mint Museum, San Francisco)

Metal Detectors

Electronic prospecting refers to locating nuggets and concentrations of black sand with its related deposits of gold by using a metal detector specifically designed for this purpose. It can be an end in itself or used as an adjunct to aid in selecting a site for any of the above methods. Additionally, it can be used in "hard rock" mining to locate the source of particularly rich veins.

Either the Beat Frequency Oscillator (BFO) or the new Very Low Frequency (VLF) type detector is used. These are employed because of their ability to produce true readings. The VLF has the ability to cancel out ground mineralization while still penetrating to satisfactory depths. Small (5-inch or less) detector search heads specifically designed for nugget hunting are offered by many manufacturers. This is a must to locate the smaller nuggets and offers maximum movement in the tight spots most likely to trap gold.

If you are interested in this method of prospecting, check the several brands that specialize in "nugget shooting." Generally, units are available in hip-mount and lightweight backpack models which add to their flexibility in the field.

Metal detectors can be an invaluable aid in desert dry washes. They eliminate the need to pan countless acres of dry, unproductive ground. By scanning placer areas in dried-up stream beds and gullies you can locate prime areas for using other equipment and locate nuggets buried under layers of sand and gravel. It is the fastest, most practical way to cover the most ground.

An advantage of the plastic pan during electronic prospecting is its use to isolate material when a reading from your detector looks promising. After a response from the metal detector's search head, a shovel is pushed as deeply as possible in the gravel to get under the source that activated the detector. Place your shovelful of paydirt into the pan and check the pan with the detector, repeating with more dirt and gravel until you discover your target.

Using a metal detector to locate deposits of black sands (magnetite) which generally also contain gold deposits. The search head can be used either on land or in shallow water.

CHAPTER V

Crescent of Gold

A t some point you will undoubtedly ask yourself, "How do I know if this is real or fool's gold?" In spite of most popular misconceptions, there is a distinct difference between the two.

Fool's gold, usually yellowish iron or copper pyrite or yellow mica, is by comparison considerably lighter in weight and will float and/or swirl with the water in your gold pan. Gold, because of its specific gravity (19.2), will move very reluctantly. Fool's gold glitters and sparkles when held in the sun; gold 'glows' and its deep yellow coloring remains so even out of direct sunlight. When touched with the tip of a knife, fool's gold, which is brittle, will flake or break. Pyrites when struck with a hammer will shatter. Gold, however, is relatively soft and malleable and can be indented, scratched and cut with a knife blade. Iron pyrite is considerably harder than gold and will not be scratched by the tip of a knife blade. It will not react when placed in nitric acid (careful, highly caustic!) while fool's gold will foam, smoke, and finally disintegrate. The best test, however, is to see some real gold. Once you have, you'll see the vast difference and never confuse the two again.

Amalgamation

During the course of your sluicing and panning experience you'll pan down to the point of picking out the larger mini-nuggets and flakes. Eventually you'll have only very fine flour gold remaining which is difficult to isolate and pick up. Depending on your level of experience and the richness of the area, you may be satisfied only with the pieces you can pick up with your tweezers, discarding the minute 'dust'. If, however, you would like to accumulate finer gold as well, there is an old-time technique that's fairly effective. It requires the use of mercury and is called *amalgamation.* You'll need a small vial of mercury, a thin chamois cloth, a medium-sized white potato, some wire and tin foil.

The affinity of gold to adhere to the mercury while rejecting most of the black sand makes this process possible. To conserve time it's best to take the material you intend to treat and accumulate it until the end of the day. The concentrate should be panned down as much as possible then put in another vessel, such as a small plastic bowl, to avoid leaving any residual mercury on your pan.

Add the mercury to the bowl of concentrate, about a teaspoon or so will do (it'll take some trial and error to judge the right amount). Gently swirl the bowl, letting the ball of mercury roll over the surface of the black sand. After you're satisfied that it has come in contact with *all* the loose gold, roll the impregnated blob onto the chamois skin which has first been soaked in water. The *amalgam,* or mixture of mercury and gold, can now be separated by closing the top of the chamois skin and turning and squeezing it to press the mercury through the pores of the skin. This should be done over another bowl to retrieve the mercury. The flour gold will not pass through the cloth. All that remains is a small 'bead' of gold.

It is essential at this point to emphasize that mercury is a deadly poison and must be treated

Osterberg's "Quick Gold" separator

85

with great care. The fumes are deadly and it must always be used *outdoors*. Contact with the skin should also be avoided and it *must not* be used at all if you have any open sores or cuts on your fingers. *Always use in a well-ventilated area.*

There is an alternate method which is popular and practical when larger amounts of black sand are accumulated such as in large sluicing or dredging operations. This method employs the use of one of the many small rotary tumblers on the market offered by lapidary manufacturers and retail stores (see list). They are extremely effective in recovering minute particles of 'flour' gold.

Generally the tumbler is used first to agitate the contents of black sand. A small amount of caustic soda is added to clean the impurities from the gold and permits the mercury (added in the second phase) to more easily adhere to *all* the gold particles. After several hours of tumbling, the mercury-impregnated gold is placed through the chamois as in the manual method. Specific directions accompany most manufacturers' equipment.

Next you'll have to remove the residual mercury from the gold. One method is to cut a potato in half lengthwise. Scoop a small pocket out of the white center large enough to hold the gold bead. Put the halves together, secure with wire and wrap in several folds of aluminum foil. The potato is then placed in a hot open *outdoor* fire to bake. *Stay away from the fire to avoid inhaling the vapors.* After an hour or so, withdraw the potato. The mercury will have been absorbed into the white meat leaving a gold lump in the pocket. *Burn, bury, or properly dispose of the potato where no person or animal will eat it.* Do not permit the bowls used in the amalgamation to come in contact with any food stuff. This old-time method is for historical information only and for safety reasons it is *not* recommended.

Gemstone's amalgamator operates on a sonic system, reclaiming fine gold trapped in heavy sands. *(Courtesy of Gemstone Equipment Manufacturing Co.)*

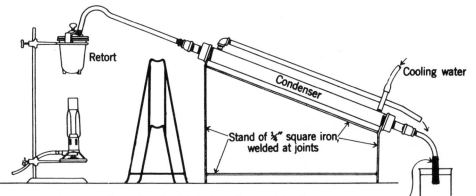

Retort

Condenser

Cooling water

Stand of ¼" square iron, welded at joints

A second method of driving the residual mercury from the gold saturated amalgam is a little more sophisticated and is called *retorting*. The *retort* works on the same principle as a still, that is, heat is used to drive off the mercury by means of distillation. The retort consists of four elements: a heat source such as a propane torch to heat the amalgam to 675 degrees, a tightly closed container to hold the amalgam, a long metal pipe which is enclosed in a water jacket to condense the vapor-ized mercury and a vessel at the terminal end to collect it.

Retort.
(Courtesy, California Division of Mines and Geology)

Retorting is relatively simple, but the unit must be properly constructed and operated to assure that none of the gases escape. Again, it must be emphasized that the equipment must be used *outdoors* to avoid the possibility of inhaling any mercury vapors. Therefore, it's important to purchase rather than build a proper retort from a mining supply house and follow their instructions carefully for its safe operation.

Significant amounts of flour gold are con-tained in the black sand. However, unless you are accumulating large amounts of *concentrate,* such as in major sluicing or dredging operations, the use of mercury will not usually justify the cost. At all times, great care must be taken while handling the mercury.

If you are planning a larger operation, however, it *definitely* pays to hang onto your accumulated black sand. Serious prospectors are aware of its value and collect every ounce for further processing, usually through mechanical rather than chemical separation. There have been several equipment developments in the last few years that warrant interest.

One device separates the black sand/gold by putting the concentrate into a state of liquid suspension, thereby isolating the gold by specific gravity. The cylindrical apparatus allows a controlled velocity of water to flow into its base section, while the concentrate is introduced into the top. A "quicksand" of suspended material floats in the clear acrylic tube, the gold drops into a trap in the bottom of the unit, while the lighter waste colloids are siphoned off.

A larger scale method employs an adapta- tion of the Archimedean screw principle of raising water (and concentrate) by means of a spiral. By adjustment of the spiral wheel's angle and spray valve, all but the heaviest elements are flushed away, thereby recovering upwards of 90% of the fine gold through the wheel's central collecting point. These machines are set up and left to do their work while the miner goes about his other operations.

The Archimedes Spiral Separator. *(Courtesy of Gemstone Equipment Manufacturing Co.)*

Staking Your Claims

If you have found a spot that *proves* to be good and you want to make an investment in time to expand the operation, you will want some assurance that someone else isn't going to start where you left off between trips. If the area is on public land, in most cases administered by the Bureau of Land Management (BLM), you can usually "stake a claim" to the mineral rights on that parcel. The governing laws vary from one state to another and within districts of the states. Dredging 'seasons' also vary to avoid any interference with fish migration and spawning seasons in certain rivers and streams. Specific information regarding details and forms for staking a claim can be obtained from the BLM office having jurisdiction over the area you are prospecting. I've listed those you are most likely to use at the end of this handbook.

Land status maps can be obtained for most areas from the local BLM office. These outline in broad forms the areas held in public domain within the area covered, and are keyed accordingly. There are, however, a number of private parcels which may not be shown because of the size of the scale. A specific area can usually be inquired about at the local ranger station. Forest rangers intimately know the terrain within their area.

Generally any U.S. citizen can "locate" and file a mining claim entitling the prospector to the mineral rights of a certain tract, usually 20 acres for an individual. The claim process usually has at least the following four elements:

1. A discovery of gold or other mineral within the boundary of the claim.
2. Erection of a monument and notice of location with description of its boundaries.

3. Clearly making the boundaries at the four corners.

4. Recordation of a true copy of the location in the appropriate county office and BLM.

    The notice of location usually contains at least the date, county, township, state and name of the claimant. The filing itself contains the same information along with a physical description of the boundaries.

    Once you have located, recorded and filed a claim with the necessary fees, marked the claim with its name, date of filing, and the name and addresses of the "holders," and meet all other local and federal requirements, you have established possessory rights to the minerals within its boundaries.

    A non-patented claim entitles the holder(s) to the mineral rights but nothing else. The public can still hunt, fish, hike, and swim there as long as it is not directly interfering with the mining operation. Annual "assessment" work is required in the performance of a specified minimum amount of mining work to keep the claim active and valid, with the necessary documents being filed in the form of a statement of proof of labor.

    As stated earlier, this is a generalized capsulation of the steps you will need to follow. Each area is governed by at least one, and usually several governmental agencies, either federal, state, local, or any combination. Begin with the local BLM and ask for their circular on current regulations. Be sure to ask what other agencies are involved (usually the Department of Fish and Game for dredging operations) and get the location of the closest ranger station within the area you wish to prospect.

    There is another point that must be stated. As the price of gold escalates to and perhaps over

the $1000 an ounce mark, there will be more and
more territorial "rights" being established to
sections of potentially profitable gold areas. In the
mountains and deserts as elsewhere, there are
some people who may be very aggressive about
protecting what they think of as "theirs," either real
or imagined. Most of these people have a legiti-
mate right to the ground they're protecting and
have spent a lot of time and money developing it.
They've also probably had the "fever" long before
gold reached its current price levels. So respect all
posted areas. There is still an awful lot of open
ground in our national forests and other federal,
state and county land. Some of it may not be right
beside a paved four-lane highway but then again
it's the most easily accessible spots that have been
worked the hardest by most people. Research and
enjoy the secondary roads and trails. That's where
the greatest rewards lie. It'll also enrich your over-
all sense of experience and appreciation of the area
you're prospecting.

TUNNELING.

CHAPTER VI

Nickel Knowledge

I n this closing section I've included a potpourri of practical information that should be helpful in your further understanding of gold and the steps leading to its recovery. Specific information and equipment should be obtained according to your individual requirements.

Survival Pack

The following is a suggested list of items that can easily fit in a small "surplus" canvas magazine or cartridge pouch, "fanny" pack or the like, in the event you get stranded. All will fit in a package no larger than 5x5x3 inches.

Compass	Energy Chocolate Bar
Snake Bite Kit	Pencil and Note Paper
Band-Aids	Fishing Hooks and
Safety Pins	50 Feet of Line
Salt Pills	Whistle
Water Purification	Signal Mirror
Tablets	Plastic Tube Tent
Matches/	15 feet Nylon Cord
"Metal" Match	Insect Repellent
Candle	"Space Blanket"

Don't	trespass on posted or fenced property.
"	prospect in national parks/monuments.
"	go off into the boonies unprepared or unfamiliar with the terrain without letting someone know where you are.
"	camp or prospect in dry washes if distant storms are prevalent; flash floods can originate from storms miles distant.
"	enter any old tunnels or shafts.
"	get discouraged!
Do	check with the department of Fish and Game regarding local ordinances.
"	have a game plan, survey the area prior to your trip to conserve time later on during your vacation.
"	look for all key spots and clues as discussed.
"	take spares of easily lost items (tweezers, vials, etc.)
"	respect posted mining claims.
"	look out for snakes sunning themselves.
"	take plenty of water if not available at your favorite mining site and drink often to avoid heat exhaustion.
"	count on your intuition. The subconscious mind can put together the ingredients and intangible evidence we've discussed for your "glory hole".

Specifications

Symbol	Au
Atomic Number	79
Atomic Weight	196.967
Melting Point	1063°C
Specific Gravity	19.2
MOH's Scale of Hardness	2.5

Sorting Your Gold By Size

To evaluate your recovery, gold is often classified by mesh size. That is, by sifting it through a screen: #10–#40 signifying each mesh's number of openings per square inch. If the gold sample passes through a particular sized screen, it is *minus*, if not, it is referred to as *plus*.

Coarse Gold — *Plus 10-mesh*. Does not pass through the mesh size but instead *remains* on a 10-mesh screen. Coarse gold, depending on its individual weight, generally is anything weighing over a "grain" and will command a premium value over the base market price as it is valued for its jewelry and collectors' appeal. Nuggets, the prospector's prize catch, are evaluated and priced individually. The margin is dependent on the specimen's size, color, character and other distinguishing features.

Medium Gold — Passes through a 10-mesh screen (*minus 10*), but remains on a 20-mesh (*plus 20*). Approximately 2,200 "colors" per troy ounce.

Fine Gold — *Minus 20-mesh* but *plus 40-mesh*. Approximately 12,000 or so colors per troy ounce. Fine gold is valued based on its assayed purity times the market price (*e.g., 1 oz. x 90% Pure x $400 per oz. = $360*).

Flour Gold — *Minus 40-mesh* and finer. Averages 40,000+ colors per ounce.

The weight of gold is always determined in *Troy* ounces as opposed to the avoirdupois scale used in most other daily commodities. The common denominator for the two scales is grains. There are 437.5 grains per avoirdupois ounce as opposed to 480 grains in one troy ounce.

Troy Weight

1 grain = 0.0648 grams

24 grains = 1 penny weight (DWT) = 1.5552 grams

20 pennyweight = 1 ounce (480 grains) = 31.10 grams

12 ounces = 1 troy lb. = 5760 grains = 373.24 grams

Laboratory Pure Gold is 1.000 Fine

Commercially Fine Gold is .999 Fine

24 Karat = 100% Pure

18 Karat = 75% Pure

14 Karat = 58% Pure

10 Karat = 42% Pure

U.S. Gold Coins are .9166 Fine (22 Karat)

	Wt/Grms	Grains Pure
Double Eagle $20	33.4370	495.0
Eagle $10	16.7185	247.50
Half Eagle $5	8.3592	123.75
Quarter Eagle $2.50	4.1796	61.875
One Dollar $1	1.6718	24.750

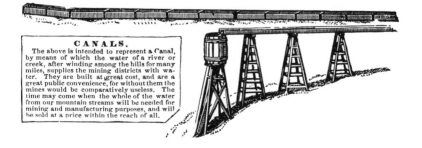

CANALS.
The above is intended to represent a Canal, by means of which the water of a river or creek, after winding among the hills for many miles, supplies the mining districts with water. They are built at great cost, and are a great public convenience, for without them the mines would be comparatively useless. The time may come when the whole of the water from our mountain streams will be needed for mining and manufacturing purposes, and will be sold at a price within the reach of all.

Notice of Location - Placer Claim

To All Whom It May Concern:

1. *The Name of the claim is* _____ *, a placer mining claim.*

2. *This claim is situated in Section* _____ *(if known or surveyed), Township* _____ *, Range* _____ *,* _____ *Meridian, in the* _____ *Mining District (if known), County of* _____ *, State of California. The acreage claimed is* _____ *acres.*

3. *The date of this location is the* _____ *day of* _____ *, 19* _____ *, on which date the notice of location was posted on the claim.*

4. *The locator or locators of this claim are:* *(current residence or mailing address)*

   Name _____ *Street* _____
   City _____ *State* _____ *Zip* _____
   Name _____ *Street* _____
   City _____ *State* _____ *Zip* _____
   Name _____ *Street* _____
   City _____ *State* _____ *Zip* _____
   Name _____ *Street* _____
   City _____ *State* _____ *Zip* _____

5. *Each locator is a citizen of the United States, or has declared intention to become such.*

6. *The locator(s) do(es) hereby locate and claim, on land embraced in the United States Public Land Surveys, the land and deposit described as the* _____
   _____ *of the above section. If not described or taken by legal subdivision description, or if on unsurveyed land, the boundaries of the claim and the land taken are described as follows:*
   Commencing at the discovery monument where this notice is posted, thence _____
   (Direction)
   _____ *to the* _____ *corner which is the point of beginning to describe the boundaries,*

   thence _____ *feet to the* _____ *corner*
   thence _____ *feet to the* _____ *corner*
   thence _____ *feet to the* _____ *corner*
   thence _____ *feet to the* _____ *corner*
   thence _____ *feet to the point of beginning.*

7. *The discovery monument is situated at the point of discovery about* _____
   _____
   _____

   (distance from natural object or permanent monument and give direction as accurately as possible, to identify the claim located)

   LOCATORS

   _____   _____

   _____   _____

Notice of Location-Lode Mining Claim

Notice is Hereby Given that:

1. The name of this claim is _____ , a lode mining claim.

2. The claim is situated in Section _____ , Township _____ , Range _____ ,
   _____ Meridian, in the _____ Mining District
   (if known), County of _____ , State of California.

3. The date of this location is the _____ day of _____ , 19 ____ ,
   on which date the notice of location was posted on the claim.

4. The locator or locators of this claim are: *(current residence or mailing address)*

   Name _____ Street _____
   City _____ State _____ Zip _____
   Name _____ Street _____
   City _____ State _____ Zip _____
   Name _____ Street _____
   City _____ State _____ Zip _____
   Name _____ Street _____
   City _____ State _____ Zip _____

5. Each locator is a citizen of the United States, or has declared intention to become such.

6. The locator(s) do(es) hereby locate and claim _____ *linear feet*
   (not to exceed 1500)
   of this vein or lode, together with surface ground extending _____
   (not to exceed 300)
   feet in width on each side of the middle of the vein or lode and more particularly described as
   follows: Commencing at the monument where this notice is posted, which monument is at the
   point of discovery on said vein or lode and on the center line of this location, _____
   (I or We)
   hereby claim _____ feet extending in a _____ direction
   along the course of the vein from the discovery monument and _____ feet
   in a _____ direction from the discovery monument, along the course of the vein.
   The general course of the vein is in a _____ erly and _____ erly direction.

7. The discovery monument is situated about _____
   _____
   _____
   _____

   (Distance from natural object or permanent monument and give directions as
   accurately as possible, to identify the claim located)

8. All dips, variations, spurs, angles, and all veins, ledges, or deposits within the lines of this claim,
   together with all water and timber and any other rights appurtenant, allowed by the laws of this
   State or of the United States are hereby claimed.

LOCATORS SIGNATURES

_____   _____

_____   _____

Cowdery's Form No. 800—Notice of Location, Lode Mining Claim (Quartz)   Rev. 8/73

A primitive outfit.
(After A Sketch
From Life In 1850,
by J. W. Audubon,
in the possession
of his daughter,
Miss M. R.
Audubon.)
*(Courtesy of The
California Historical
Society, San
Francisco)*

Building and Operating
Your Own Rocker Box

For those of you who are interested in fabricating some of your own equipment, as did the early miners, I included plans for the construction of a "Rocker Box." The plans are basic and proportions can be modified to suit individual needs as to size, weight, and types of wood and other materials. A ruler, saw, drill, assorted screws, nuts and bolts, wood and canvas/corduroy material and related tools are about all you'll need. Your own ingenuity will allow you to modify the construction (let's say with wing nuts where applicable) should you want to be able to breakdown and reconstruct the rocker for easier transport in the field.

The basic reasons for the development of the gold rocker are the same today as when it was originally developed in the gold fields of the 1800's. It is the natural conclusion of the combined experience of thousands of working miners; it will wash the most gravel *with the least amount of water* at the highest rate of recovery. The serious miner can therefore use this tool as a quick and reliable means of analyzing test holes during the course of evaluating a prospective area, while the more casual argonaut will find the gold rocker easy to use and many times faster than the gold pan for small scale recovery.

Operation of the "Gold Rocker"

The rocker basket, or hopper, is first half filled with gold-bearing dirt or gravel. With a dipper or other container, water is then poured over the dirt while the hopper is rattled back and forth by short rapid jerks on the handle. A slow and steady stream of water best ensures that the gold will settle out and not be washed away with the lighter materials.

The separation of gold takes place at progressive stages during its course of travel through the box. All the gold, dirt and small rocks are washed through the holes in the bottom of the hopper, leaving oversized rocks in the hopper to be discarded before the hopper is refilled.

After passing through the holes, the material falls on the upper portion of the canvas apron and flows into the apron pocket which acts as a nugget trap. This pocket catches most of the larger and some of the smaller pieces of gold while the lighter materials are floated over the lip of the pocket and into the riffle box below. The accumulations in the apron can be emptied periodically and tested in the pan to determine the value of the ground being worked.

The riffle box consists of a sloping chute with two linings on the bottom – one of corduroy or burlap and an overlying one of wire mesh. These linings are held in place by a series of "riffle" bars whose rungs are at right angles to the flow of water and act as barriers to the suspended materials being washed through the box. As with the apron pocket above, the lighter dirt washes over these riffles, while the gold, being heavier, remains trapped behind them and in the lining. At the end of the day, the lining is carefully removed and washed clean and the days collection of gold reclaimed.

To do this, the screws and/or wing nuts holding the riffle assembly and linings are removed. Next, after placing a gold pan or bucket of sufficient size at the mouth of the box, water is poured into the empty hopper, gently washing the riffle ladder, wire mesh, and corduroy one by one before removing from the box. Make sure that all gold-bearing materials are washed into the box and from there into the gold pan without spilling. These concentrates are then washed in the pan and then panned out in the usual manner.

As in the operation of the sluice box, you'll have a large quantity of "concentrates," which should be panned out slowly to capture all the gold contained within.

Prospectors using pans, rockers and sluices tore up miles of riverbanks and streambeds in their search for gold

SIERRA "GOLD RUSH" ROCKER

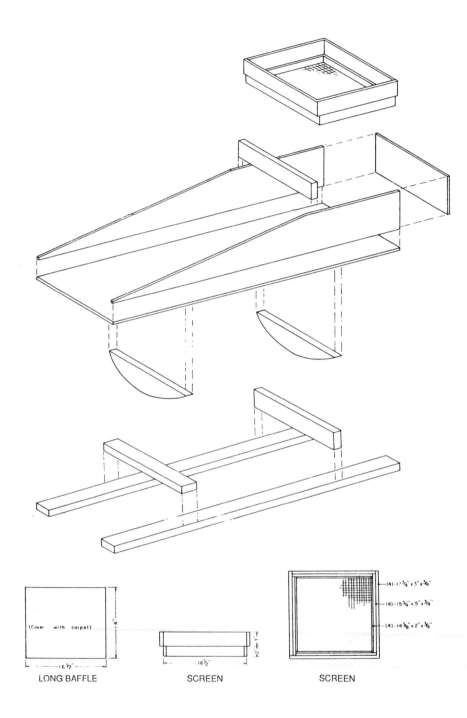

(Cover with carpet)

14

16 ½"

LONG BAFFLE

16 ½"

2 ½"

SCREEN

(4)-1"x ¾" x 3" x ¾"

(4)-15 ¾" x 5" x ¾"

(4)-14 ⅜" x 2" x ¾"

SCREEN

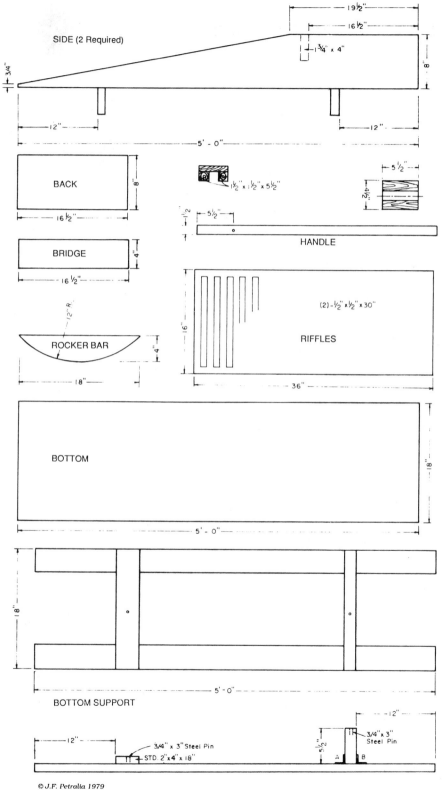

SIDE (2 Required)

19½"

16½"

1¾" x 4"

8"

3/4"

12"

12"

5' - 0"

BACK

8"

16½"

½" x ½" x 5½"

5½"

4½"

BRIDGE

4"

16½"

½"

5½"

HANDLE

2" R.

ROCKER BAR

4"

18"

16"

(2) -½" x ½" x 30"

RIFFLES

36"

BOTTOM

18"

5' - 0"

18"

5' - 0"

BOTTOM SUPPORT

12"

12"

3/4" x 3" Steel Pin

3/4" x 3" Steel Pin

STD. 2"x4" x 18"

5½"

A   B

© J.F. Petralia 1979

103

CHAPTER VII

Where To Prospect

Is There Any Gold Left? *Yes!...*for a number of reasons: for one, as explained earlier, the very nature of the process of Mother Nature's concentrating gold over eons in ancient river channels and the subsequent directing and erosive recutting of new water courses has released only a small percentage of the gold that their tertiary rivers contain. Also, in the normal course of events, wind, rain and seismic activity have allowed erosion from the lode gold source to replenish the same streams that held such a bonanza for the early '49ers.

Look at the headlines in the regions of the historic mining towns such as Jamestown or Downieville after a particularly heavy spring run-off: "Gold Fever [again] strikes the Motherlode!" Every few years either a heavy snow-pack run-off or ideally a warm, heavy, late season rain on a thick snowpack will cause a river or stream to virtually overrun its banks; in the process the water, rocks and boulders will abrade and scrape away tons of new auriferous materials from the sides of the earth. As it cuts the ancient river channels that it bisects, so it frees and transports fresh gold down river until the streambed can no longer support the gold's weight in suspension. Then as its waters recede, gold is redeposited anew.

The story goes, in the mountains, that when an extremely high water run-off occurs, you can literally hear the huge boulders clanging and banging into each other as the river rocks and gravels are rearranged. The next few days, as the river recedes, offer prime times for walking the river's course and "sniping" for the fresh nuggets it left behind.

There also are areas that were too difficult to mine effectively in the early days because the high walls and narrow canyons would not allow the original argonauts to divert the stream from its course. These areas are *prime* for today's gold dredges. Bench placers and dry washes were also sometimes considered unproductive either because the methodology to process the hills was outlawed (hydraulicking) or the wide diversity in gold occurrence, due to the infrequent yet high volume or velocity of an infrequent runoff of a semi-arid area, made the result too sporadic for a consistent payout. The available technology of electronic prospecting often times makes these areas virgin ground for the 20th century "miner." Consider also that many areas formerly mined have been left untouched for over a hundred years. The ensuing earthquakes, landslides, floods, etc., have released a renewed supply of gold to these regions.

Whether you favor panning, sluicing, dredging, dry-washing, sniping or electronic prospecting, there are thousands of locations across the country to prospect. What follows are some of the most famous and those that offer the most potential for the part-time prospector.

Gold Concentrations in the U.S.

The rules of the game remain the same regardless of where you plan to prospect. You first have to select the general area that you plan to work and then research its history. The areas that produced best in the past are continuingly replenishing themselves and likely will contain enough values to make it worthwhile for the recreational prospector. Check with the Bureau of Land Management's regional office for information on specific areas, including geological maps that depict the mineral deposits, topographical maps outlining the area's key features, and access and reference sketches on major discoveries. Check the historical section of the county libraries for the background on local areas' mining activity.

The point to keep in mind is that while an area may have been heavily worked in the past, commercial operations have lost interest in many of these areas, and therefore they can be very profitable to an individual with modern equipment. Also, many of these places have been idle for a long time. In the ensuing years, gold has continued to erode from its source by weathering, floods have washed away host material and gravels, and stream courses have been reshifted by nature—all contributing to the renewal of the resource.

What follows is but the tip of the proverbial iceberg. It offers simply a taste of where to begin your search. It is meant only to give you a head-start and point you in the right direction so that you can focus on an area that is convenient or is of interest to you. Reference material is available both on a regional and state-by-state basis from most mining supply resources to help guide you to the most productive areas.

The Southeast
Alabama — Shortly after gold was discovered in Georgia in 1828, strikes were made in Alabama. These were worked for over ten years before the mining activity was abandoned early on as the prospectors headed to the richer strikes in California. The placer fields worked in the early 19th century have been virtually idle since. Check the histories of Clay, Randolph, Cleburne and

Tallapoosa Counties; in particular the deposits around Gold Hill and in the Clear Creek area in the Arbacoochee District, in Cleburne County, and the drainage and lode areas around Hog Mountain in Tallapoosa County.

Georgia — Abandoned by her miners in the "Rush of '49," Georgia produced enough gold in its heyday to warrant a U.S. Mint at Dahlonega. Coins with its mint mark are rare, prized collectors' items today. The namesake of the town's early mint and its surrounding creeks, as well as the placers of White County, are a haven for weekend prospectors.

North Carolina — The oldest recording of gold discovery in the then United States (not what is now the United States, as the early Spaniards discovered gold throughout the southwest) was in North Carolina. Gold was discovered there in 1799. The principal locations for today's adventurer lie in South Mountain's Brindletown Placers, Cabarrus County (the original discovery site), the Portis Placers of Franklin County, a short section of the Uwharrie River located in Montgomery County and Randolph County, the placer deposits of Uncon and Stanley Counties, and the Georgetown Creek gravels located in Transylvania County.

South Carolina — Although there was considerable production in the years preceding the Civil War, mining has been mostly idle since the turn of the century. Investigate the history of the northwestern section of Chesterfield County, Lancaster County and McCormick County, if that is the area most convenient to your home base.

Virginia — Again, discovered early in this country's history, Virginia offers some interesting locations, which were the sites of early placer mining activity, in which to try your luck. Namely: Busby Creek in Fluvanna County, also in Spotsylvania, Orange and Faquier Counties.

Western States

Arizona — Riddled with tales of lost gold mines, Arizona has a rich and colorful history of lode and placer discoveries. Cochise County has recorded over two and a half million ounces of gold from lode production, but is relatively poor in placer deposits. Appreciable amounts of gold come out of Mohave, Pima, Yavapai and Yuma Counties. The Bisbee, Dos Cabezas, Tombstone, Turquoise, Gila, Banner, Ask Peak, Clifton-Morenci, Vulture, San Francisco, Wallapai, Ajo, Mammoth, Pinal County, Ray, Superior, Big Bus, Maricopa, Pingrove-Tiger Districts have yielded vast amounts of gold, but they have either come from hardrock lode operations or as a by-product from copper, sulfide ore, or silver production.

The more interesting areas for the modern-day prospector would be the following: Bisbee District, Ash Canyon in the Huachuaca Mountains, Barbarossa and Payson Placers, the latter in Gila County; the Globe-Miami District, the San Domingo Placers and Vulture District in Maricopa County; Pina County's Alder Canyon; Armargosa, Baboquivari, Papago and Quijotoa Placers; the placer areas in Yavapal County include Granite Creek, Groom Creek, Placerita Placer and the Weaver-Rich Hill District; the LaPaz and Plomosa District, LaCholla Placer, and Muggins Mountain area of Yuma County.

California — Where do we begin? This is literally the motherlode of all gold producing regions of the United States. More importantly, it is an amateur's (as well as a professional's) dream, since most of its gold production comes from relatively easy-to-reach placer deposits. To go county-by-county, enumerating each creek, gulch, stream or bench in which gold can be found, would take another complete book or two. For the sake of brevity, I've listed only the most productive and popular areas. There is a ton of reference and historical material available, to keep anyone busy for years, at state, county and local libraries, universities and government offices that documents virtually any area in which you're interested.

The richness of the California motherlode has been attributed to the gradual erosion and subsequent accumulation of gold from ancient rivers, of major proportions, that ran in a south-southeasterly direction through the central part of the state. The forces that formed the earth, moved and broke-up her super continents and formed her mountains, displaced the ancient rivers. The rivers and streams, that subsequently cut at right angles through the mountains of the Sierra Nevada, are believed to have cut through the fabled Big Blue Lead and other tertiary river channels and carry its rich treasure.

These other ancient river channels are theorized to have been off-shoots, tributaries if the word is appropriate for so large a river system, from a "super" river. The theory being that before the break-up of the continents, the ancient, monster water channel ran all the way from what is now the South American coastline, up through Mexico and through the western corridor to Canada; each tilting and breaking of its old path further segmenting its branches and obscuring more of its original course. Where these channels were forced closest to the surface and not protected by ancient lava flows, the canyons and fissures that cut into it released its mineral wealth. It is therefore the drainages of the western slope of the Sierras that have always attracted the most interest.

The major rivers to consider for panning, sluicing and dredging often cross over into more than one county. Some areas are obviously more productive than others for the circumstances that led to the gold-bearing quartz "source" veins, which originate deep within the earth, being closer to the surface, and, thus eroded, its alluvial and placer is concentrated more in some areas than others. These are obviously the areas that you'll want to concentrate your efforts on as they'll produce the most return for your labor. Also, keep your *eyes peeled* for sections of ancient streambed or "benches" that are isolated from the present day's river's course. Also, keep a sharp eye out for any nuggets that may have wedged themselves into tight, exposed fissures. It is not uncommon to find these after the high water recedes, with or without the aid of a metal detector.

All of the following rivers and areas that are listed below will produce sufficient "color" to begin your search, from the drainages of the western flank of the Sierras and its major rivers and their forks as well as the creeks and other tributaries that feed them, followed by whatever other area intrigues you:

The American River—its middle fork in El Dorado County, above the Rubicon River; its south fork above Chili bar as well as Rock Creek; its North Fork in the Weimar/Colfax areas as well as Duncan and Shirttail Canyon and the Bear River in Placer County. The Consumnes River and its north fork near Martinez Creek as well as Deer Creek, the Indian Diggings District's tertiary gravels, likewise the placer gravels east of Placerville in the Pacific District and those of Pilot Hill and Placerville itself, again in El Dorado County. The tributaries of the San Joaquin River including the Consumnes, Mokelumne, Calaveras, Stanislaus, Tuolumne and Merced Rivers and their feeder creeks. In Trinity County, the Trinity River and Willow Creek and the other drainages that form it, Canyon Creek outside the town of Weaverville, The Klamath and

Salmon Rivers; Cherry, Indian, McAdam, French and Deadwood Creeks, of the latter, plus Humbug Creek outside of the Town of Yreka. The French Gulch Mining District north of the Town of Redding in Shasta County, Bee Gum Gulch near the site of Platina and Clear, Flat and Oregon Creeks off the Sacramento River; Cottonwood Creek and its tributaries of Antelope, Crow and Roaring Creek.

In Butte County, the drainages of the tertiary channel near the Cherokee mining area, the Feather River's south fork near Forbestown, and Butte, Hon Cut and Wilson Creeks.

The north fork of the Yuba River between Sierra City and Downieville, the confluence of the Downie and North Yuba below town, and Sailors Ravine, Wolf, Kanaka, Fiddle, Good and Lavazzola Creeks in Sierra County. The district around the neighboring cities of Grass Valley and Nevada City. This area is riddled with mine shafts and tunnels for its rich lode deposits and the area is surrounded by bench deposits, many of which have never been hydraulicked. The drainage and creeks around this region are also replete with vast untouched tertiary gravel deposits and the natural effects of erosion are constantly replenishing them as well as the placers of the south fork of the Yuba River and nearby Deer Creek.

The Dry Creek and Gold Beach Park area, the old gravel deposits of Forest Home near Ione, Jackson Creek in the Pine Grove District, the creeks and streams around the site of West Point east of Pine Grove Hill located in Amador County.

In Calaveras County: Calaveritas Creek, the Mokelumne Hill District and Rich Gulch area, as well as the tertiary channel drainages near Calaveritas. Maxwell Creek near Coulterville, the placers in the Cathay Valley District and the Merced River outside of Yosemite. Colorado Creek and Mariposa

Creek around the town of Coulterville in Mariposa County. Tuolumne County's Wood Creek near Jamestown, the so-called ancient Cataract River channel near Calaveras Grove and near Douglas Flat, as well as Big Hum Bug Creek and the water courses washing the areas around the old mining camps of Groveland, Garrotte and Deer Flat, and the creeks and streams around Jamestown.

In the southern tip of the state there is the Kern River and its placer deposits, the dry washings in the gulches of the Rand Mountains around the site of Stinger. A section of the Chowchilla River near Raymond, San Bernardino County's Holcomb Creek in the valley of the same name, the north slope drainages of the Old Dad Mountains, as well as the Whipple Mountains located northeast of Vidal Junction. Northeast of Los Angles there is the east fork of the San Gabriel River, north of Azuza where I first cut my teeth panning, Bear Canyon and Haskell Canyon north of Saugus, and if you still have time, having thoroughly explored and prospected all of the above, there's the Piute Mountains, Black Gulch, Bradshaw, Freemont and Greenhorn Creeks in the Greenhorn Mountain, and for the dry-washing aficionados the canyons of Red Rock, Goler, Summit, Garlock and, appropriately, Last Chance, in the El Paso range.

Colorado — Second only to California, this centrally located Rocky Mountain state affords many opportunities for today's amateur prospector. Boulder County produced well over a million ounces of gold, but most of that was credited to lode operations or by-products of other minerals being mined. Check out the creeks and streams draining the Front Range as well as the headwaters of the Arkansas and South Platte Rivers. Chaffee County's better placer producers include the Arkansas River, Cottonwood, Clear,

Cache and Pine Creeks, Lost Canyon, Gison Gulch, Oregon Gulch and Ritchey's Patch; Gilpin County's Northern Gilpin and Central City District; Taylor River and the Gold Brick–Quartz Creek area of Gunnison County; Clear Creek in Jefferson County; Lake County offers rich prospects in the Arkansas River and the tributaries that feed it, including Box and Lake Creeks; the La Plata Mountain area in the county of same name; Park County has good potential and a number of areas to prospect including the eastern range of the Mesquite Mountains in the Alma District; Beaver and Sacramento Creeks and the South Platte River in the Fairplay District; Summit County's Georgia Gulch placer.

Idaho — Originally a significant producer of placer gold, Idaho turned to lode production after the turn of the century, when gold was either the main or by-product focus of its mining activities. For our purposes, the areas of the most interest are in Boise County's rivers and streams; the Caribou Mountain region of Bonneville County; Clearwater Creek in Clearwater County; check the rivers and streams in Custer County, in particular those of Loon Creek, Jordan Creek, south fork of the Boise River and Bear Creek, the latter located in the Rocky Bar District; Idaho County's Newsome Creek; the Snake River in the Power and Bingham County area; Latah County's HooDoo Mountain area, including the Palouse River, and lastly the rich potential of Lemhi County, the latter being concentrated in the Carmen Creek, Gibbonsville, Mackinaw and Texas Districts and the waterways contained therein, namely: Carmen, Eldorado, Sandy, Pratt, Hirtley, Napias and Boulder Creeks.

Montana — A consistent producer for the modern-day prospector, the southwestern area of the state is laced with excellent placer regions. Focusing on these areas, Broadwater County is among the richest, specifically the tributaries of

Confederate Gulch on the Missouri River; Crow Creek and Johnny Gulch in the Radersburg District; the Avalanche, White Creek and Magpie Gulch area in the White Creek District; and some placer returns from Beaver Creek in the Winston District. Research the northern section of the First Chance District, Henderson Creek in Henderson district, both in Granite County; Lewis and Clark Countys' tributaries of the Blackfoot River, Last Chance Gulch near the City of Helena, the drainage creeks on the western slopes of the Belt Mountains, Silver Creek, Ten Mile Creek, the Stemple Pass area including Virginia Creek's placers; Madison County's Alder Gulch and the Virginia City District; Elk Creek in Missoula County. Also worth the time to investigate are the eastern drainages of the Bitterroots in Mineral County and the placers of Missoula, Park, Powell and Ravalli Counties, and the headwater placers of the Clark Fork of the Columbia River.

Nevada — Renown as the Silver State, Nevada produces a large amount of gold as well. Be prepared, however, for an arid climate and limited water for your mining activities. The better areas for the amateur prospector are: Douglas County, in the Pine Nut Mountains on Buckeye Creek; in Elko County, placer deposits along Columbia, Sheridan and Blue Jacket Creeks, Grasshopper Gulch north of Mt. City, Coleman and Hammond Canyon including, of course, Gold Creek, the south fork of the Owyhee River and Van Duzer Creek; the placers west of Lida, southwest of Tonopah; the drainages and creeks northwest of Carlin in the Lynn District of Eureka County; the Battle Mountain and Shoshone Peak drainages and gulches of Mill and Triplett including Mud Spring Gulch located near Tenabo, all located in Lander County; the Raw Hide wash diggings and the tributaries to it, located southeast of the Town of Fallon; Nye

County's Cloverdale Creek, placer deposits of the
Manhattan District of the Toquima Range, as well
as the richer deposits located on Round Mountain's
western slopes; the placer areas of Rabbit Hole
Creek, the canyons of Sacramento, Weaver,
Rochester, Limerick and Rose Bud, the Sierra District's rich placer deposits, the extensive placers of
the canyon regions in the western half of the state
named American and South American, and Troy
Canyon in the Spring Valley District in the Hum-
boldt Range, all located in Pershing County.

New Mexico — The early explorers prospected around the southwest hundreds of years ago.
Although no reliable records have survived, it is
generally understood that a considerable amount of
the precious metal was recovered. Here's a sampling
of prospective areas: the major drainages of Mount
Baldy, namely Ute and Willow Creeks as well as the
South Pontil, Anniseta, Mills and the other gulches
of the Moreno River, all in Colfax County; Grant
County's central district, as well as Bear Creek and
Santo Domingo Gulch near the early settlement of
Pinos Altos; the south and central drainages and
related placers of the Big Burro Mountains; the
Jicarilla Mountains, particularly the gulches Ancho,
Rico, Spring and Warner. Placer and El Rito Creeks
in Rio Arriba County. In Santa Fe County the wes-
tern San Pedro Mountain region's Tuerto Creek and
its tributaries, as well as Lazarus Gulch and Cun-
ningham Gulch, the latter in the vicinity of the Town
of Dolores; the gulches around Anomas Hills, near
Hillsboro including Gold Run and Little Gold Run,
Hunkidori, Dutch and Green Horn in Sierra County;
the Rio Grande River's bars and Placer and Cabresto
Creeks, near the Red River; and the Canyons of
Lama, Alamo and Garrapata in Taos County were
all early sites of the Spaniards' efforts. Also note-
worthy are the placer deposits found in Orogrande,
Hopewell and the Millsboro Mining Districts.

Oregon — Baker County in eastern Oregon around Auburn including the Connor Creek area and Burnt River areas, the tributaries leading into the Powder River and the Morman Basin District Southeast of Bridgeport; Grant County's drainages and creeks of the John Day River, and its north fork; Granite Creek after the town and district of the same name and surrounding creeks; Dixie Creek, southwest of Green Horn; Jackson County gave up its first discovery just several years after gold was discovered in California, this includes Jackson Creek and the tributaries to the Upper Applegate River, and color can be found in the streams around Gold Hill; Josephine County in the Golice District, below the confluence of Josephine Creek and the Illinois River, the better known tributaries of the lower Applegate River including Williams, Oscar, and Slate Creeks, also in Josephine County; the drainages of the Blue and Wallows Mountains in the northeast part of the state and streams draining the Klamath Mountains in the southwest region of Oregon.

South Dakota — The history and culture of our country might be considerably different had there not been gold discovered in the Black Hills. (Remember Custer's troop sent out to defend the miners?) Lawrence County's Deadwood District, the drainages around Ragged Top, Elk Mountain, Carbonate and the central section around Lead should prove of interest; Pennington County's placers, though inconsistent, were probably never tapped to their full potential and modern prospecting techniques could yield good results.

Utah — Although the major part of Utah's gold production is a by-product of other mining activities, it has enough significantly important placers to be of some interest to the recreational prospector. Crescent Creek in Garfield County is worth checking out if you want to try your hand at dry-washing; Grand County's Colorado River placers offer up some very fine gold, also the drainages of the North LaSal Mountains; Tooele County's Camp Floyd District's placer deposits and those of the Willow Springs District; the Green River in the Horseshoe Bend area of Unitah County's Split Mountain Gorge; the American Fork District just southeast of Cottonwood.

Washington — Rich in rivers that erode and classify the gravels, there are some areas worth putting some time into to check out. Peshastin Creek near the town of Wenatchee; the drainages to the northeast of Chelan County's mid-point, and the Entiat River; likewise, the drainages in the area of the Town of Republic; Okanogan County's Myer's and Granite Creek, Mary Ann Creek and the placer deposits around Palmer Mountain; Whatcom County's Ruby and Slate Creeks and the placers of the Western drainage of the Cascade should also be explored.

Wyoming — Most of the gold recovered in Wyoming is a by-product of other mining activities, but this is a big, thinly populated state and bears further investigation, particularly in the Douglas Creek area of Albany County and in the area south of Lander in Fremont County.

Alaska

Second only to California in the multiplicity of areas in which gold is found, Alaska provides one of the best areas for the amateur prospector. Gold has been found, with varying degrees of concentration, in most of Alaska's streams and rivers and even in some of its beach sands. Bear in mind, however, that Alaska contains very little in the way of paved roads, or any roads at all for that matter, outside of the routes between its largest cities. What it lacks in convenience, for the modern miner, it more than makes up for in adventure in the truest sense of what it must have been like for the early miners in the way of isolation and excitement. The area is vast and the weather and environment, in general, can cause a lot of problems for the unprepared. If you do plan to "strike it north," then do your homework! Research the area's history, work out your transportation and other logistics beforehand.

The best known areas which have been explored and contain the richest placering areas include the placer deposits of the Yukon River basin as well as deposits in the rivers and tributaries draining the following: The Districts of Aniak, Anvik, Bethel, Bonnifield, Chandalar, Chisana, Chistochina, Circle, Council, Eagle, Fairbanks, Fairhaven, Fortymile, Hope, Hot Springs, Hughes, Iditarod, Innoko, Kantisha, Kougarou, Koyok, Koyukuk, Juneau, Marshall, McGrath, Nizina, Nome, Rampart, Ruby, Shugnak, Tolouana, Valdez and Yentna.

Freight wagons being staged at Yale, British Columbia.

118

Head for the Hills!

The recreational recovery of gold is a hobby enjoyed by thousands for the pure pleasure of being outdoors in country you might not normally visit. It's a trip into the past to an earlier time in this country's history, to the towns that were formed because of the richness of the surrounding soil. A day, a weekend, a vacation, or a camping holiday can be formed around this activity – the total experience being the sum of its parts. However, unlike other outdoor activities such as fishing and hunting, you or the people you mention your hobby to will invariably ask: What is it worth? How much did you find? Did it pay for the trip? I guess this is natural because of the universal awareness of the 'value' of gold.

You have to consider a couple of things in your own mind regarding its worth. Are you in it for the sport or for profit? If you are doing it for the fun of it, a guide to its estimated value would be helpful. On the other hand, if you're pursuing this as labor for its monetary remuneration because of the potential profit, you'll soon escalate your involvement into a considerable amount of equipment and capital, including precise instruments to measure the amount of gold recovered.

For the recreational prospector, some examples may be helpful. A day in a good area, using a sluice, can produce a yield from several grains to a couple of pennyweight, one pennyweight being $\frac{1}{20}$ of a troy ounce. At today's prices that can add up pretty quickly. A Kruggerand, which is one troy ounce of gold, is approximately the size of a half dollar but slightly thicker. If you mentally cut up the surface area of that coin in fractions of a quarter or less, you can 'ballpark' the amount you've found. Inexpensive scales ($20-25) that are fairly precise for the price are available at supply houses.

Once you begin finding pieces in the nugget category, technically any piece of gold that weighs more than a grain (480 to the troy ounce) but generally anything from a half pennyweight on up, you will begin to appreciate more of a return than from "fine" gold. These pieces can be used for jewelry in the form of earrings, pendants and ring mounts, and command prices from a minimum of twice the spot price on up several times, depending on the size, texture, and character of the nugget. Pieces that have quartz mixed in with the

Off to the "diggings." *(Photo courtesy of Southern Pacific Transportation Co.)*

metal are particularly desirable, with varying value in proportion to the formation, tint, and amount of quartz. These specimen pieces are highly prized by collectors and are somewhat rare.

The grains and dust you find can be displayed in the small vials available at variety stores, encapsulated in small, clear plastic spheres available at jewelry stores, and hung as pendants. The "fines" can also be melted together to make a unique freeform piece of jewelry.

If you accumulate enough gold and wish to sell it, contact one of the refiners of precious metals in the Yellow Pages. Be sure to hold aside the "nugget" pieces. They will not be worth any more to the refiner whose only concern is to melt them together with the rest into large castings for resale.

Once you begin your quest, in all likelihood it will open and expand your interest into an exciting new endeavor. It will spur your interest in the history of our recent past, the geology of the area, and the details of the hills and mountains that surround us all. The search for that shining, elusive metal will be both exciting and frustrating but through it all will be a rich experience you will not soon forget, nor will it leave you unchanged.

Using gold prospecting, perhaps as an excuse, I have ventured and adventured into places that I would never have otherwise explored. Prospecting for gold is a *pro-active* hobby. The planning, anticipation and actuation all add depth and dimension to the adventure. An old Asian proverb says, "*A journey is its own reward...*" The "journey" will take you and your friends to areas that you might not otherwise have explored...So, enjoy it—that's what life's about!

Good Luck!

*(Photo courtesy of
Levi Strauss & Co.)*

Additional Reading

- *The Ancient River of Gold* — RAYMOND WALLACE

- *Dredging for Gold* — MATT THORNTON

- *Dry Washing for Gold* — JAMES KLEIN

- *Forty Niners* — ARCHER BUTLER HULBERT

- *Geological Guidebook Along Highway 49 (California Division of Mines, Bulletin #141)* — OLAF P. JENKINS

- *Gold Locations of the United States* — JACK BLACK

- *Gold Placers of California (California Mining Bureau Bulletin #92)* — CHARLES HALEY

- *Guide to Gold Panning in British Columbia* — N.L. BARLEE

- *The Modern Gold Seekers Manual* — TOM BRYANT

- *Prospecting for Gold* — GRANVILLE STUART

- *Sierra County: Volumes I–IV* — JAMES J. SINNOTT

- *Stake Your Claim* — MARK S. SILVA

- *Tertiary Gravels of the Sierra Nevada of California* — WALDEMAR LINDGREN

- *U.S. Department of the Interior, Geological Survey; Denver's Geological Setting*

- *The World Rushed In* — J. S. HOLLIDAY

Bureau of Land Management (BLM) Offices

Alaska State Office
555 Cordova Street
Anchorage, AK 99501
(907) 277-1561

Arizona State Office
2400 Valley Bank Center
Phoenix, AZ 85073
(602) 261-3873

California State Office
Federal Building
Sacramento, CA 95825
(916) 484-4676

Colorado State Office
Colorado State Bank Building
Denver, CO 80202
(303) 837-4325

Eastern States Office
(All states east of Mississippi River)
7981 Eastern Avenue
Silver Springs, MD 20910
(301) 427-7500

Idaho State Office
Federal Building
Boise, ID 83724
(208) 384-1401

Montana State Office
(Montana, North and South Dakota)
Granite Tower Building
222 N. 32nd Street
Billings, MT 59101
(406) 657-6461

Nevada State Office
Federal Building
Reno, NV 59609
(702) 784-5451

New Mexico State Office
(New Mexico, Oklahoma, and Texas)
Federal Building
Santa Fe, NM 87501

Oregon State Office
(Oregon & Washington)
729 N.E. Oregon Street
Portland, OR 97208

Utah State Office
University Club Building
136 E. South Temple Street
Salt Lake City, UT 84111
(801) 524-5311

Wyoming State Office
(Wyoming, Nebraska, and Kansas)
Federal Building
Cheyenne, WY 82001
(307) 778-2326

Notes/Potential Mining Sites

Location:

    State _____

    County _____

    Coordinates _____

Type of Deposit:

    Place _____

    Bench _____

    Lode _____

Distinctive Features:

_____

_____

_____

Historical Background:

_____

_____

_____

Sampling Results:

_____

_____

_____

Miscellaneous Data:

    Altitude _____

    Season _____

    Water level _____

    Accessibility _____

Sketch:

Glossary

Amalgam—The combined mass of the mixture of mercury and gold and/or other metals.

Amalgamation—The use of mercury to collect fine gold from the final washed down concentrate.

Atomic Number—A number representing the weight of one atom of an element as compared with an arbitrarily selected number representing the weight of another element taken as the standard.

Arrastre—A mechanical device consisting of a yoke and millstone usually turned by mule power in the early days of mining to crush rock and separate the gold.

Auriferous—Ground or material bearing or yielding gold.

Bar/Gravel Bar—A deposit of gravel and rock usually caused by the slower currents of water in streams and rivers, and associated with gold, where present.

Bed Rock—The solid underlying layer beneath gold-bearing gravels and just above the alluvium soil zone to which the gold cannot further pass.

Bench—A terrace of gravel along the bank of a stream left by the action of the water in earlier times.

Black Sand—Concentrations of the heavy minerals of magnetite, limonite, chromite, hematite and the like whose discovery usually indicates the source, where present, of other heavy metals, i.e. gold.

Bullion—Molded bars or ingots of gold (or other precious metals) that have been smelted and refined to a specified pure state, generally .99+ Fine.

Claim—The fixed area of land, defined by specific boundaries, its assignment legally affixed [hence "claimed"] for the retrieval of its presumed mineral content.

Claim Jumping—Stealing someone else's mining claim before it's been recorded or, nowadays, the use during the owner's absence.

Colors—The particles of gold amid the black sand left in the gold pan after washing.

Coyoteing/Coyote Holes—The practice of sinking a

shaft or tunnel large enough for one man to crawl into while following the path of a rich "vein" of gold.

Dredge— Either a large, floating barge processing unit that withdraws auriferous material via a bucket type device and washes the gravels of gold, or, more commonly nowadays, a mechanically driven suction device that sucks up material from stream and river bottoms and separates it through a sluice.

Dredging— The use of a subsurface hose powered by an engine to suck up auriferous material which is in turn separated in the sluice portion of the equipment.

Dry Washer— A mechanical device for separating the gravels and soil from the gold without the use of water.

Fool's Gold— Mineral sometimes mistaken for gold, made up of iron sulfide or copper-iron sulfides and often yellow or brass in color.

Glory Hole— A relatively small but concentrated pocket of gold.

Gold Fever— A disease, when contracted, having no known cure; periods of dormancy sometimes occur in winter months. Symptoms include a faraway look, a "need" to get into the mountains, an expanded love of the outdoors, and an endless search for the buried location of the pot at the end of the rainbow.

Grain— Originally derived from the weight of a single grain of wheat, the smallest unit in the system of weights and measures.

Gravel Bar— A deposit of gravel-sized rock formed by the slower current or diminished velocity of water in either a stream or river.

Grubstake— Supplying a prospector with "grub" and equipment for a percentage of his take.

Hydraulicking— The practice, now outlawed or severely restricted in most areas, of directing a high-pressure stream of water at benches and river banks to wash the material into sluices and "Long Toms" to recover gold.

Ledge—A horizontal layer or deposition of gold-bearing materials.

Lode— A deposit or vein containing quantities of valuable mineral mined by digging a tunnel or sinking a shaft. [see vein]

Long Tom— A large, usually wooden trough used in the early days of mining in which gold-bearing material and water were used to separate the gold from the gravels.

Motherlode— The main "lode" or vein of ore; the general region having a considerable quantity of auriferous material, referred to as the central mining district on the western flanks of the Sierra range.

Nugget— A lump or small mass of gold (or silver) in its native state.

Outcrop—An exposed surface of a vein, lode or other mineral deposit.

Patent—The written transfer of title by the government to the claimee, after the latter has complied with a number of obligations to satisfy his claim.

Paydirt— Soil, gravel, ores, etc., rich enough in minerals to make mining profitable.

Pay Streak or "Lead"— A concentrated area or layer of placer gold.

Placer— A deposit of gravel or sand containing heavy ore minerals including gold which has eroded from the surrounding mountains.

Quartz— A hexagonal crystalline material often colorless or milk-white and associated with gold "veins."

Rocker— Early invention in the general shape of a cradle which combined the aspects of a sluice with a section built in its forward section to sort out the rocks.

Stamp Mill— Any number of designs used to crush ore and separate the gold from the host material.

Tailings — The waste material from a former mining operation consisting of processed gravels and rock left as a waste product and often containing gold missed by the former operation.

Troy Ounce — A specific weight measurement designation for weighing silver and gold. One troy ounce is equal to 1.097 Avoirdupois ounces.

Vein— A rich, clearly defined tabular, mineralized ore deposit, generally in a hardrock source. *[see lode]*

Wingdam— Obstruction constructed to divert water to or away from a mining operation.

Appendix

HEADQUARTERS TENTH MILITARY DEPARTMENT
Monterey, California, August 17, 1848.

SIR: I have the honor to inform you that, accompanied by Lieutenant W. T. Sherman, 3d artillery, acting assistant adjutant general, I started on the 12th of June last to make a tour through the northern part of California. My principal purpose, however, was to visit the newly-discovered gold placer in the valley of the Sacramento.

I had proceeded about forty miles when I was overtaken by an express, bringing me intelligence of the arrival at Monterey of the United States store ship Southampton, with important letters from Commodore Shubrick and Lieutenant Colonel Burton. I returned at once to Monterey, and despatched what business was most important, and on the 17th resumed my journey. We reached San Francisco on the 20th, and found that all, or nearly all, its male population had gone to the mines. The town, which a few months before was so busy and thriving, was then almost deserted. On the evening of the 24th, the horses of the escort were crossed to Sansolito in a launch, and on the following day we resumed the journey, by way of Bodega and Sonoma, to Sutter's Fort, where we arrived on the morning of the 2d of July. Along the whole route mills were lying idle, fields of wheat were open to cattle and horses, houses vacant, and farms going to waste. At Sutter's there was more life and business. Launches were discharging their cargoes at the river, and carts were hauling goods to the fort, where already were established several stores, a hotel, &c. Captain Sutter had only two mechanics in his employ—a wagon-maker and blacksmith—whom he was then paying ten dollars per day. Merchants pay him a monthly rent of one hundred dollars per room, and whilst I was there a two-story house in the fort was rented as a hotel for five hundred dollars a month.

At the urgent solicitation of many gentlemen, I delayed there to participate in the first public celebration of our national anniversary at that fort, but on the 5th resumed the journey and proceeded twenty-five miles up the American Fork, to a point on it now known as the lower mines, or Mormon diggings. The hill sides were thickly strewn with canvass tents and bush arbors. A store was erected, and several boarding shanties in operation. The day was intensely hot, yet about two hundred men were at work in the full glare of the sun, washing for gold, some with tin pans, some with close-woven Indian baskets, but the greater part had a rude machine known as the cradle. This is on rockers six or eight feet long, open at the foot, and at its head has a coarse grate and sieve; the bottom is rounded, with small cleets nailed across. Four men are required to work this machine; one digs the gravel in the bank close by the stream, another carries it to the cradle and empties it on the grate, a third gives a violent rocking motion to the machine, whilst a fourth dashes water on from the stream itself. The sieve keeps the coarse stones from entering the cradle, the current of water washes off the earthy matter, and the gravel is gradually carried out at the foot of the machine, leaving the gold mixed with a fine heavy black sand above the first cleets. The sand and gold, mixed together, are then drawn off through auger holes into a pan below, are dried in the sun, and

---

* As printed in House Ex. Doc. 17, 31st Cong., 1st sess., pp. 529-536, 1850. Colonel Mason was commanding officer of the United States forces in California, and acting governor.

afterwards separated by blowing off the sand. A party of four men thus employed at the lower mines averaged a hundred dollars a day. The Indians, and those who have nothing but pans or willow baskets, gradually wash out the earth and separate the gravel by hand, leaving nothing but the gold mixed with sand, which is separated in the manner before described. The gold in the lower mines is in fine bright scales, of which I sent several specimens.

As we ascended the south branch of the American Fork, the country became more broken and mountainous, and at the saw-mill, twenty-five miles above the lower washings, or fifty miles from Sutter's, the hills rise to about a thousand feet above the level of the Sacramento plain. Here a species of pine occurs, which led to the discovery of the gold. Captain Sutter, feeling the great want of lumber, contracted, in September last, with a Mr. Marshall, to build a saw-mill at that place. It was erected in the course of the past winter and spring—a dam and race constructed; but when the water was let on the wheel, the tail race was found to be too narrow to permit the water to escape with sufficient rapidity. Mr. Marshall, to save labor, let the water directly into the race, with a strong current, so as to wash it wider and deeper. He effected his purpose, and a large bed of mud and gravel was carried to the foot of the race. One day Mr. Marshall, when walking down the race to this deposite of mud, observed some glittering particles at its upper edge: he gathered a few, examined them, and became satisfied of their value. He then went to the fort, told Captain Sutter of his discovery, and they agreed to keep it secret until a certain grist-mill of Sutter's was finished. It however got out, and spread like magic. Remarkable success attended the labors of the first explorers, and in a few weeks hundreds of men were drawn thither. At the time of my visit, but little more than three months after its first discovery, it was estimated that upwards of four thousand people were employed. At the mill there is a fine deposite, or bank of gravel, which the people respect as the property of Captain Sutter, although he pretends to no right to it, and would be perfectly satisfied with the simple promise of a pre-emption, on account of the mill which he has built there, at considerable cost. Mr. Marshall was living near the mill, and informed me that many persons were employed above and below him, and they used the same machines as at the lower washings, and that their success was about the same, ranging from one to three ounces of gold per man daily. This gold too is in scales, a little coarser than those of the lower mines. From the mills Mr. Marshall guided me up the mountain, on the opposite or north bank of the South Fork, where, in the beds of small streams, or ravines, now dry, a great deal of the coarse gold has been found. I there saw several parties at work, all of whom were doing very well. A great many specimens were shown me, some as heavy as four or five ounces in weight; and I send three pieces, labelled No. 5, presented by a Mr. Spence. You will perceive that some of the specimens accompanying this hold, mechanically, pieces of quartz, that the surface is rough, and evidently moulded in the crevice of a rock. This gold cannot have been carried far by water, but must have remained near where it was deposited from the rock that once bound it. I inquired of many people if they had encountered the metal in its matrix, but in every instance they said they had not, but that the gold was invariably mixed with washed gravel, or lodged in the crevices of other rocks. All bore testimony that they had found gold in greater or less quantities in the numerous small gullies or ravines that occur in that mountainous region. On the 7th of July I left the mill and crossed to a small stream emptying into the American Fork, three or four miles below the saw-mill. I struck this stream (now known as Weber's creek) at the washings of Suñal & Co. They had about thirty Indians employed, whom they pay in merchandise. They were getting gold of a character similar to that found in the main fork, and doubtless in sufficient quantities to satisfy them. I send you a small specimen, presented by this company, of their gold. From this point we proceeded up the stream about eight miles, where we found a great many people and Indians; some engaged in the bed of the stream, and others in the small side valleys that put into it. These latter were exceedingly rich, and two ounces were considered an ordinary yield for a day's work. A small gutter, not more than a hundred yards long by four feet wide and two or three feet deep, was pointed out to me as the one where two men, William Daly and Perry McCoon, had, a short time before, obtained in seven days $17,000 worth of gold.

Captain Weber informed me that he knew that these two men had employed four white men and about a hundred Indians, and that, at the end of one week's work, they paid off their party and had left with $10,000 worth of this gold. Another small ravine was shown me, from which had been taken $12,000 worth of gold. Hundreds of similar ravines, to all appearances, are as yet untouched. I could not have credited these reports had I not seen, in the abundance of the precious metal, evidence of their truth. Mr. Neligh, an agent of Commodore Stockton, had been at work about three weeks in the neighborhood, and showed me, in bags and bottles, over $2,000 worth of gold; and Mr. Lyman, a gentleman of education and worthy of every credit, said he had been engaged, with four others, with a machine, on the American Fork, just below Sutter's saw-mill, that they worked eight days, and that his share was at the rate of fifty dollars a day; but, hearing that others were doing better at Weber's place, they had removed there, and were then on the point of resuming operations.

I might tell of hundreds of similar instances; but to illustrate how plentiful the gold was in the pockets of common laborers, I will mention a simple occurrence which took place in my presence when I was at Weber's store. This store was nothing but an arbor of bushes, under which he had exposed for sale goods and groceries suited to his customers. A man came in, picked up a box of seidlitz powders, and asked its price. Captain Weber told him it was not for sale. The man offered an ounce of gold, but Captain Weber told him it only cost fifty cents, and he did not wish to sell it. The man then offered an ounce and a half, when Captain Weber *had* to take it. The prices of all things are high; and yet Indians, who before hardly knew what a breech-cloth was, can now afford to buy the most gaudy dresses.

The country, on either side of Weber's creek, is much broken up by hills, and is intersected in every direction by small streams or ravines, which contain more or less gold. Those that have been worked are barely scratched, and, although thousands of ounces have been carried away, I do not consider that a serious impression has been made upon the whole. Every day was developing new and rich deposites, and the only apprehension seemed to be that the metal would be found in such abundance as seriously to depreciate in value.

On the 8th of July I returned to the lower mines, and on the following day to Sutter's, where, on the 10th, I was making preparations for a visit to the Feather, Yubah, and Bear rivers, when I received a letter from Commodore A. R. Long, United States navy, who had just arrived at San Francisco from Mazatlan, with a crew for the sloop-of-war Warren, and with orders to take that vessel to the squadron at La Paz. Captain Long wrote to me that the Mexican Congress had adjourned without ratifying the treaty of peace, that he had letters for me from Commodore Jones, and that his orders were to sail with the Warren on or before the 20th of July. In consequence of these, I determined to return to Monterey, and accordingly arrived here on the 17th of July. Before leaving Sutter's, I satisfied myself that gold exists in the bed of the Feather river, in the Yubah, and Bear, and in many of the small streams that lie between the latter and the American Fork; also, that it had been found in the Cosumnes, to the south of the American Fork. In each of those streams the gold is found in small scales, whereas in the intervening mountains it occurs in coarse lumps.

Mr. Sinclair, whose rancho is three miles above Sutter's, on the north side of the American, employs about fifty Indians on the North Fork, not far from its junction with the main stream. He had been engaged about five weeks when I saw him, and up to that time his Indians had used simply closely-woven willow baskets. His nett proceeds (which I saw) were about $16,000 worth of gold. He showed me the proceeds of his last week's work—fourteen pounds avoirdupois of clean washed gold.

The principal store at Sutter's Fort, that of Brannant & Co., had received in payment for goods $36,000 worth of this gold from the 1st of May to the 10th of July; other merchants had also made extensive sales. Large quantities of goods were daily sent forward to the mines, as the Indians, heretofore so poor and degraded, have suddenly become consumers of the luxuries of life. I before mentioned that the greater part of the farmers and rancheros had abandoned their fields to go to the mines; this is not the case with Captain Sutter, who was carefully gathering his wheat, estimated at 40,000 bushels. Flour is already worth at Sutter's $36 a barrel, and soon will be fifty. Unless large quantities of breadstuffs reach the country, much suffering will occur; but as each man is now able to pay a large price, it is believed the merchants will bring from Chili and Oregon a plentiful supply for the coming winter.

The most moderate estimate I could obtain from men acquainted with the subject was, that upwards of four thousand men were working in the gold district, of whom more than half were Indians, and that from $30,000 to $50,000 worth of gold, if not more, was daily obtained. The entire gold district, with very few exceptions of grants made some years ago by the American authorities is on land belonging to the United States. It was a matter of serious reflection with me how I could secure to the government certain rents or fees for the privilege of procuring this gold; but upon considering the large extent of country, the character of the people engaged, and the small force at my command, I resolved not to interfere, but permit all to work freely, unless broils and crimes should call for interference. I was surprised to learn that crime of any kind was very unfrequent, and that no thefts or robberies had been committed in the gold district. All live in tents, in bush houses, or in the open air, and men have frequently about their persons thousands of dollars' worth of this gold; and it was to me a matter of surprise that so peaceful and quiet a state of things should continue to exist. Conflicting claims to particular spots of ground may cause collisions, but they will be rare, as the extent of the country is so great, and the gold so abundant, that for the present there is room and enough for all; still the government is entitled to rents for this land, and immediate steps should be devised to collect them, for the longer it is delayed the more difficult it will become. One plan I would suggest is to send out from the United States surveyors, with high salaries, bound to serve specified periods; a superintendent to be appointed at Sutter's Fort, with power to grant licenses to work a spot of ground, say 100 yards square, for one year, at a rent of from $100 to $1,000, at his discretion; the surveyors to measure the grounds and place the renter in possession. A better plan, however, will be to have the district surveyed and sold at public auction to the highest bidder, in small parcels, say from 20 to 40 acres. In either case, there will be many intruders, whom for years it will be almost impossible to exclude.

The discovery of these vast deposites of gold has entirely changed the character of Upper California. Its people, before engaged in cultivating their small patches of ground and guarding their herds of cattle and horses, have all gone to the mines, or are on their way thither; laborers of every trade have left their work-brenches, and tradesmen their shops; sailors desert their ships as fast as they arrive on the coast, and several vessels have gone to sea with hardly enough hands to spread a sail; two or three are now at anchor in San Francisco with no crews on board. Many desertions, too, have taken place from the garrisons within the influence of the mines; 26 soldiers have deserted from the post of Sonoma, 24 from that of San Francisco, and 24 from Monterey. For a few days the evil appeared so threatening that great danger existed that the garrisons would leave in a body; and I refer you to my orders of the 25th of July to show the steps adopted to meet this contingency. I shall spare no exertions to apprehend and punish deserters; but I believe no time in the history of our country has presented such temptations to desert as now exist in California. The danger of apprehension is small, and the prospect of higher wages certain; pay and bounties are trifles, as laboring men at the mines can now earn in *one day* more than double a soldier's pay and allowances for a month, and even the pay of a lieutenant or captain cannot hire a servant. A carpenter or mechanic would not listen to an offer of less than fifteen or twenty dollars a day. Could any combination of affairs try a man's fidelity more than this? And I really think some extraordinary mark of favor should be given to those soldiers who remain faithful to their flag throughout this tempting crisis. No officer can now live in California on his pay. Money has so little value, the prices of necessary articles of clothing and subsistence are so exorbitant, and labor so high, that to hire a cook or servant has become an impossibility, save to those who are earning from thirty to fifty dollars a day. This state of things cannot last forever; yet, from the geographical position of California, and the new character it has assumed as a mining country, prices of labor will always be high, and will hold out temptations to desert. I therefore have to report, if the government wish to prevent desertions here on the part of men, and to secure zeal on the part of officers, their pay must be increased very materially. Soldiers both of the volunteer and regular service discharged in this country should be permitted at once to locate their land warrants in the gold district. Many private letters have gone to the United States giving accounts of the vast quantity of gold recently discovered, and it may be a matter of surprise why I have made no report on this subject at an earlier date. The reason is, that I could not bring myself to believe the reports that I heard of the wealth of the gold district until I visited it myself. I have no hesitation now in saying that there is more gold in the country drained by the Sacramento and San Joaquin rivers than will pay the cost of the present war with Mexico a hundred times over. No capital is required to obtain this gold, as the laboring man wants nothing but his pick, shovel, and tin pan, with which to dig and wash the gravel; and many frequently pick gold out of the crevices of rock with their butcher knives in pieces from one to six ounces.

Mr. Dye, a gentleman residing in Monterey, and worthy of every credit, has just returned from Feather river. He tells me that the company to which he belonged worked seven weeks and two days, with an average of fifty Indians, (washers,) and that their gross product was 273 pounds of gold. His share, one-seventh, after paying all expenses, is about 37 pounds, which he brought with him and exhibits in Monterey. I see no laboring man from the mines who does not show his two, three, or four pounds of gold. A soldier of the artillery company returned here a few days ago from the mines, having been absent on furlough twenty days; he made by trading and working during that time $1,500. During these twenty days he was travelling ten or eleven days, leaving but a week, in which he made a sum of money greater than he receives in pay, clothes, and rations during a whole enlistment of five years. These statements appear incredible, but they are true.

Gold is believed also to exist on the eastern slopes of the Sierra Nevada; and when at the mines, I was informed by an intelligent Mormon that it had been found near the Great Salt lake by some of his fraternity. Nearly all the Mormons are leaving California to go to the Salt lake, and this they surely would not do unless they were sure of finding gold there in the same abundance as they now do on the Sacramento.

The gold "placer" near the mission of San Fernando has long been known, but has been but little wrought for want of water. This is a spur that puts off from the Sierra Nevada, (see Fremont's map,) the same in which the present mines occur. There is, therefore, every reason to believe that in the intervening space of five hundred miles (entirely unexplored) there must be many hidden and rich deposites.

The placer gold is now substituted as currency of this country; in trade it passes freely at $16 per ounce; as an article of commerce its value is not yet fixed. The only purchase I made was of the specimen No. 7, which I got of Mr. Neligh at $12 the ounce. That is about the present cash value in the country, although it has been sold for less. The great demand for goods and provisions made by this sudden development of wealth has increased the amount of commerce at San Francisco very much, and it will continue to increase.

I would recommend that a mint be established at some eligible point on the bay of San Francisco, and that machinery, and all the apparatus and workmen, be sent by sea. These workmen must be bound by high wages, and even bonds, to secure their faithful services; else the whole plan may be frustrated by their going to the mines as soon as they arrive in California. If this course be not adopted, gold to the amount of many millions of dollars will pass yearly to other countries, to enrich their merchants and capitalists. Before leaving the subject of mines, I will mention that on my return from Sacramento, I touched at New Almoden, the quicksilver mine of Mr. Alexander Forbes, consul of her Britannic Majesty at Tepic. This mine is in a spur of mountains 1,000 feet above the level of the bay of San Francisco, and is distant in a southern direction from the Pueblo San Jose about twelve miles. The ore (cinnabar) occurs in a large vein dipping at a strong angle to the horizon. Mexican miners are employed in working it, by driving shafts and galleries about six feet by seven, following the vein.

The fragments of rock and ore are removed on the backs of Indians in raw-hide sacks. The ore is then hauled in an ox wagon from the mouth of the mine down to a valley well supplied with wood and water, in which the furnaces are situated. These furnaces are of the simplest construction, exactly like a common bake-oven, in the crown of which is inserted a whaler's trying kettle; another inverted kettle forms the lid. From a hole in the lid a small brick channel leads to an apartment or chamber, in the bottom of which is inserted a small iron kettle. This chamber has a chimney.

In the morning of each day the kettles are filled with mineral, (broken in small pieces,) mixed with lime; fire is then applied, and kept up all day. The mercury, volatilized, passes into the chamber, is condensed on the sides and bottom of the chamber, and flows into the pot prepared for it. No water is used to condense the mercury.

During a visit I made last spring, four such ovens were in operation, and yielded in the two days I was there 656 pounds of quicksilver, worth at Mazatlan $1.80 per lb. Mr. Walkinshaw, the gentleman now in charge of this mine, tells me that the vein is improving, and that he can afford to keep his people employed even in these extraordinary times. This mine is very valuable of itself, and becomes the more so, as mercury is extensively used in obtaining gold. It is not at present used in California for that purpose, but will be at some future time. When I was at this mine last spring, other parties were engaged in searching for veins; but none have been discovered that are worth following up, although the earth in that whole range of hills is highly discolored, indicating the presence of this ore. I send several beautiful specimens, properly labelled. The amount of quicksilver in Mr. Forbes's vats on the 15th of July was about 25,000 pounds.

I enclose you herewith sketches of the country through which I passed, indicating the position of the mines, and the topography of the country in the vicinity of those I visited.

Some of the specimens of gold accompanying this were presented for transmission to the department by the gentlemen named below; the number on the topographical sketch, corresponding to the numbers on the labels of the respective specimens, show from what part of the gold region they were obtained:

1. Captain J. A. Sutter.
2. John Sinclair.
3. William Glover, R. C. Kirby, Ira Blanchard, Levi Fairfield, Franklin H. Ayer; Mormon diggings.
4. Chas. Weber.
5. Robert Spence.
6. Sernal & Co.
7. Robert D. Neligh.
8. C. E. Picket; American Fork, Columa.
9. E. C. Kemble.
10. T. H. Green, from San Fernando, near Los Angeles.
A. Two ounces purchased from Mr. Neligh.
B. Sand found in washing gold, which contains small particles.
11. Captain Frisbie; Dry diggings, Weber's creek.
12. Cosumnes.
13. Cosumnes; Hartnell's ranch.
14. A small specimen, supposed to be platina, found mixed with the finer particles of the gold.

I have the honor to be your obedient servant,

R. B. Mason,
Colonel 1st Dragoons, commanding
General R. Jones, *Adjutant General U.S.A., Washington, D.C.*

Mining Supply Resources

The following is a cross-section of some of the prospecting supply retailers nationwide that carry mining and lapidary equipment as well as books and maps. This is by no means a complete list nor does the omission of a dealer's name indicate that he is not reliable. Check your Yellow Pages under *Mining—Supplies* for a local dealer or write to one of those listed below (★ = *distributor*) for their catalog.

Alaska

Alaska Mining & Diving Supply
    3222 Commercial Drive
    Anchorage, AK 99501

Alaskan Prospectors
    504 College Road
    Fairbanks, AK 99701

Arizona

A&B Prospecting Supplies
    3929 E. Main, #32
    Mesa, AZ 85206

Arizona Gold 'n' Treasures
    1878 E. Apache Blvd.
    Tempe, AZ 85281

DeTorres Detectors
    2008 11th Ave.
    Yuma, AZ 85364

Desert Trails
    5025 E. 29th Street
    Tucson, AZ 85711

Gold-N-Silver
    2065 Highway 95, Suite 71
    Bullhead City, AZ 86442

Many Feathers Books & Maps
    2626 West Indian School Road
    Phoenix, AZ 85017

Morey Dector Sales
    3818 E. Hardy
    Tucson, AZ 85716

Placer Equipment Inc.
    3068 N. 30th Avenue
    Phoenix, AZ 85017

★Pro-Mack Mining Supplies South
    940 West Apache Trail
    Apache Junction, AZ 85220
    (800) 722-6463

21st Century Prospector
    2047 Northern Avenue
    Kingman, AZ 86401

California

Alleghany Supply Co.
    910 Upper Main St.
    Alleghany, CA 95910

Axiom Coin & Precious Metals
    314 E Street
    Chula Visa, CA 92010

Azusa Gold
    615 Azusa Ave.
    Azzusa, CA 91702

Bill's Electronics
    984-D East Street
    Chico, CA 95926

Binkley's ARC Lapidary
    2202 Lincoln Ave.
    San Jose, CA 95125

Cal Gold Enterprises
    2569 E. Colorado Blvd.
    Pasadena, CA 91107

California Prospecting Co.
    7906 LaPalma
    Buena Park, CA 90620

Carmel Bay Mining Co.
    27383 Schulte Road
    Carmel, CA 93923

Columbia Concrete Pumping
    18169 Main Street
    Jamestown, CA 95310

Falk Elect. & Prospecting Supplies
    832 Barstow
    Clovis, CA 93612

★Fisher Research Laboratory
    200 W. Willmott Road
    Los Banos, CA 93635
    (209) 826-3292

Fortyniner Mining Supply
    16238 Lakewood Blvd.
    Bellflower, CA 90706

Fumble Fingers
1027 Brown Ave.
Lafayette, CA 94549

Gems Galore
240 Castro Street
Mt. View, CA 94041

Gold Prospecting Expeditions
18170 Main Street
Jamestown, CA 95327

Gold Seekers
6044 Skyway
Paradise, CA 95969

The Grizzly Mining Co.
P.O. Box 1478
Jamestown, CA 95327

House of Treasure Hunters
5714 El Cajon Blvd.
San Diego, CA 92115

★Jimmy Sierra Mining
3095 Kerner Blvd.
San Rafael, CA 94901
(415) 456-0891

K's Tumblecraft
223 N. Magnolia
El Cajon, CA 92020

★Keene Engineering Inc.
9330 Corbin Avenue
Northridge, CA 91324
(818) 993-0411

Marconi's Mining Supply
23400 E. Ford Rd.
Azusa, CA 91702

The Metal Smythe
152 Sacramento St.
Auburn, CA 95603

Mining and Lapidary Ind.
131 10th Street
San Francisco, CA 94103

Mother Lode Dive Shop
2020 "H" Street
Sacramento, CA 95814

Pioneer Mining Supplies
943 Lincoln Way
Auburn, CA 95603

★Pro-Mack Mining Supplies North
62832 Highway 9 / P.O. Box 47
Happy Camp, CA 96039
(800) 992-6463
(916) 542-6463

Prospector's Claim
2124 First Street
Livermore, CA 94550

Prospector's Equipment & Service
8440 Cerrittos Ave., #8
Stanton, CA 90680

Prospector's Trading Post
P.O. Box 126
Columbia, CA 95310

Riviera Coins and Stamps
1505 S. Pacific Coast Hwy.
Redondo Beach, CA 90277

Sacramento Coin Exchange
8548 Madison Ave.
Fair Oaks, CA 95626

Sieler's Sierra Gold
651 Main Street
Downieville, CA 95936

Stan and Pat's Gold Pan
247 Orchard Ave.
Vacaville, CA 95688

Stapp Mining
1295 N. "E" Street
San Bernardino, CA 92404

T.C. Mining Suplpy
3318 Santa Fe St.
Riverbank, CA 95367

Trinity Mining Supply Co.
404 Main Street
P.O. Box 1053
Weaverville, CA 96093

Colorado

Chipita Gems
8825 US Hwy 24 W
Chipita Park, CO 89809

Colorado Metal Detector Sales
311 Royal Gorge Blvd.
Canon City, CO 81212

Homestead Sports Center
11238 West US Hwy 50
Poncha Springs, CO 81242

The Prospector's Cache
3461 S. Broadway
Englewood, CO 80110

Connecticut

Lucky Strike Rock Shop
283 N. Washington St.
Plainville, CT 06062

Florida

★Kellyco Detector Distributors
1085 W. Belle Avenue
Winter Springs, FL 32708
(800) 327-9697

Reilly's Treasured Gold
2003 W. McNab Road, #10
Pompano Beach, FL 33069

Tanner's Metal Detectors
3135 S. Florida Ave.
Lakeland, FL 33803

Georgia

Buck's Marine & Gold
 Public Square, 201 S.C. St.
 Dahlonega, GA 30533
Crisson Gold Mine
 Rt. 5 Box 805
 Dahlonega, GA 30533
East Coast Prospecting & Mining
 Rt. 3 Box 321 "J" Airport RD.
 Ellijay, GA 30540
Gold & Gem Grubbin'
 Rt. 3, Box 3040
 Cleveland, GA 30528
The Gold Shop
 #8 Public Square
 Dahlonega, GA 30533

Idaho

Bob's Prospecting Supplies
 1414 Ripon, P.O. Box 671
 Lewiston, ID 83501
Idaho Stamp and Coin
 3506 Rose Hill
 Boise, ID 83705

Missouri

Bob's Treasure Unlimited
 9716 Brook Lane
 Raytown, MO 64133
Bolce's Golden Eagle Metal Det.
 5856 Hampton Ave.
 St. Louis, MO 63109
★ Plateau Detector Center
 9837 Kimker
 St. Louis, MO 63127

Montana

Montana Mining Supply, KEI
 33 Spanish View Drive
 Bozeman, MT 59715
The Prospector's Shop
 6312 Highway 12 W.
 Helena, MT 59601

Nevada

Action Mining
 4460 W. Reno Ave., #D
 Las Vegas, NV 89118
Golden Horde
 85 C St., #B / P.O. Box 755
 Virginia City, NV 89440
Highway 50-95 Rock Shop
 4261 Reno Hwy.
 Fallon, NV 89406
Marge & Al Supply
 411 S. 5th
 Box 2325
 Elko, NV 89801

Reno Prospectors Supply
 315 Caremont Street
 Reno, NV 89502

New Hampshire

Streeter Electronics
 14 Mt. Vernon
 Keene, NH 03431

New Mexico

Kohl's Rock Shop
 942 Eubank NE
 Albuquerque, NM 87112

New York

Jerry's Treasure Den
 527 Charles Ave., Geddes Plaza
 Syracuse, NY 13209

North Carolina

Cotton Patch Gold Mine
 Rural Route 3, Box 335
 New London, NC 28127
Treasure Hutch
 6960 Barkwood Dr.
 Lewisville, NC 27023

Ohio

White's of The Great Lakes
 6626 Monroe Street, Suite C
 Sylvan, OH 43560

Oklahoma

Arrowhead Supply
 330 S.W. 28th
 Oklahoma City, OK 73109
Trans-Mississippi Electronics
 905 N. Yale Ave.
 Tulsa, OK 74115

Oregon

Armadillo Mining Shop
 2041 N.W. Vine St.
 Grants Pass, OR 97526
★ Compass Electronics
 3700 24th Avenue
 Forest Grove, OR 97116
D & K Detector Sales
 13809 S.E. Division
 Portland, OR 97263
G. S. & C. Sports Shop
 2428 NE Broadway
 Portland, OR 97232
Le Bleu's Rock Shop
 1810 N.E. Stephens
 Roseburg, OR 97470
Lynn Von Blumenstein's
Treasure Hunter Outdoor Sales
 611 Lancaster Dr. NE
 Salem, OR 97301

Spence Mining and Supply
2700 Broadway
Baker, OR 97814

★ White's Metal Detectors
1011 Pleasant Valley Road.
Sweet Home, OR 97386

South Carolina

Mr. Jim's Rocks and Minerals
409 Westbrook Court
Spartanburg, SC 29303

Texas

Alexander Enterprises
1101 College Ave.
So. Houston, TX 77587

★ Garrett Electronics, Inc.
2814 National Drive
Garland, TX 75041

Research & Recovery Int'l.
2803 Old Spanish Trail
Houston, TX 77054

Treasure Hunter's Supply
1819 6th St. North
Texas City, TX 77590

Texas Treasure Hunting
5604 River Oaks Blvd.
Ft. Worth, TX 76114

Treasure Cove
100-A W. Camp, Wisdom Rd.
Duncanville, TX 75116

Whitaker Electronics
5904 Samuell Blvd.
Dallas, TX 75228

Utah

Eureka Prospecting Supplies
5585 S. 320 W
Salt Lake City, UT 84111

The Gold Digger
253 N. Main St.
Moab, UT 84532

Hardrock Ricks ProspectingSupplies
4419 S. 2950 East
Salt Lake City, UT 84124

Rocky Mountain Prospector Supplies
153 N. State, Orem Plaza
Orem, UT 84057

Vermont

Leisure Line
RD 3 Woodstock Ave./Box 7340
Rutland, VT 05701

Virginia

Blue Ridge Dive & Craft Shop
1726 Allied St.
Charlottesville, VA 22901

Washington

Bowen's Hideout
South 1823 Mt. Vernon
Spokane, WA 99223

Doug's Prospecting
13710 NE 20th Street
Bellevue, WA 98005

Glencourt Electronics
3508 Nob Hill Blvd.
Yakima, WA 98902

Int'l. Prospectors Supply
312 Dexter Ave. North
Seattle, WA 98109

Lortone Inc. – Lapidary Equip. Mfr.
2856 N.W. Market St.
Seattle, WA 98107

New WestProspecting Supply
HCR-72
Loomis, WA 98827

Nugget Bucket
5849 Hudson Lane
Ferndale, WA 98248

Wisconsin

★ Outdoor Outfitters
705 Elm St.
Waukesa, WI 53186
(414) 542-4435

Australia

Treasure Ent. of Australia
50 Henley St. , Coopers Plains
Queensland 4108, Australia

Canada

Goldfinder Canada Ltd.
11 Belmount Dr., St. Albert
Alberta , Canada T8NOC3

Rock Mountain Detectors Ltd.
P.O. Box 5366, Postal Station "A"
Calgary, Alberta, Canada, T2H-1X8

Clubs and Organizations

▶ Modern Gold Miner & Treasure Hunters Assoc./ The New 49ers Prospecting Club
Southern Chapter: 940 W. Apache Trail, Apache Junction, AZ 85220 (602) 983-3484
Northern Chapter: P. O. Box 47, Happy Camp, CA 96039   (916) 493-2062

▶ Gold Prospectors Association of America
P.O. Box 507, Bonsall, CA 92003   (619) 728-6620

Mining Supplies

The following equipment are the basic "tools"
of the modern prospector and can be ordered
directly from: Sierra Trading Post, P.O. Box 2497,
San Francisco, California 94126-2497. Please order
early as supplies become limited during the peak
spring/summer mining season.

Medium Size Gold Pan*
Advanced design, high impact plastic with built-in
steep riffles, textured surface, non-corrosive and
lightweight. Three sets of riffles incorporate three
different surface areas to help you classify and
separate your gold faster and more efficiently.
Green in color to contrast against the gold.
(14-inch diameter)   **Price: $12.95**

Gold Pan Sieve*
High impact plastic with #4-mesh stainless steel
screen. This can be used with any type of gold pan
that is approximately the same size or larger or can
be stacked on top of a 5-gallon bucket. Screens out
waste gravel to cut panning or sluicing time in half!
(approx. 10-inch diameter)   **Price: $12.95**

Mini-Sluice
Light-weight aluminum construction, features
removable riffles, diamond expanded screen, and
DuPont® matting. Approx. 10 x 36 inches – 5 lbs.
(9 ½ lbs. shipping weight)   **Price: $69.95**

Hand-Sluice
Aluminum construction with removable riffles,
diamond expanded screen for ultra fine gold
recovery, lined with DuPont® matting. Approx.
10 x 52 inches – 11 lbs. (15 lbs. Shipping weight)
Price: $89.95

Gold Scale*
Its unique design comes in a velvet-lined case.
Attractive brass scale includes a set of troy weights
to accurately weigh your gold.   **Price: $49.95**

Hydraulic Concentrators

This unit's unique hopper/sluice box design can either be used in its primary configuration as a "high-banker" to wash placer deposits some distance above stream level or from a water source, or with the addition of the optional 2½-inch power-jet suction nozzle, it can operate as a portable suction dredge. *The ultimate in a portable, efficient gold recovery machine!*

S/173 – Powered by a 3 HP Briggs & Stratton engine and complete with P-103 Pump, FVA 15-foot valve/hose assembly and 25 feet of 1-inch pressure hose. *82 lbs. (102 lbs. shipping weight)*   **Price: $875.00**

S/173-25 – Deluxe dredge conversion model (similar to illustration on p.77) contains an additional 10 feet of 2½-inch suction hose, a 2½-inch dredge suction nozzle, and 12½ feet of additional pressure hose. *98 lbs. (118 lbs. shipping weight)*   **Price: $975.00**

Backpack Dredge

This is the most economical, powerful and lightweight 2-inch dredge on the market! Features a custom-built, heavy duty 2 HP engine weighing only 9 lbs. and an all-aluminum pump which produces 90 gallons per minute. The new inflatable pontoons can be rolled up and the aluminum frame can be disassembled for a compact package for backpacking. Capable of dredging up to 2 cubic yards per hour, this dredge can be equipped with either a 2-inch power-jet, which is ideal for most conditions and provides the most suction, or a 2-inch suction nozzle for use in extremely shallow water conditions. It also can be set up or operated on the bank without using the flotation tube.

S/2003-PJ with Power-Jet   **Price: $899.00**
45 lbs. (56 lbs. shipping weight)

S/2003-SN with Suction Nozzle   **Price: $899.00**
45 lbs. (56 lbs. shipping weight)

S/2001 with suction nozzle   **Price: $875.00**
for shallow water dredging and inner tube flotation in lieu of pontoons. *40 lbs. (46 lbs. shipping weight)* *(illustrated on page 78)*

Prospector's Special

Get started with all the proper equipment in one package — and SAVE!

This kit has all the basic tools to get you started.
Great for backpacking, weekend trips and vacationers!

ONLY $49.95

- **Gold Pan**
- **Classifier Sieve**
- **Combination Pick / Mattock**
- **Crevice Tool**
- **Magnifying / Specimen Box**
- **Black Sand / Gold Separator**
- **1oz. Gold Sample Vial**

(9 lbs. shipping weight)

Order Form

NAME OF ARTICLE	QUANTITY	PRICE	TOTAL
			$

MAIL ORDER TO:
Sierra Trading Post
P.O. Box 2497
San Francisco
CA 94126-2497B

Subtotal: $ _____

California Residents add 7½% Sales Tax: _____

Postage & Handling: _____

Total Enclosed: $ _____

ORDERED BY _____

STREET ADDRESS *(NO P.O. BOXES — WE SHIP VIA UPS)*

TOWN/CITY _____ STATE _____ ZIP _____

Order Early! Please allow approximately 2–3 weeks for delivery.

Please print all information clearly so your order may be filled promptly. Minimum order is $25.00.

Please send cashiers check or money order. Personal checks take approximately 7–10 banking days to clear. No C.O.D.s. We ship via UPS which requires a street address. (UPS will not ship to P.O. Boxes)

Shipping Instructions:

All prices are F.O.B. San Francisco, California. Shipping cost is additional. For smaller equipment, marked with an asterisk (*), send $3.75 for postage. For other items add $2.50 for first pound and $0.75 for each additional pound for postage and handling.

Due to changes of material cost beyond our control, prices are subject to change without notice.

Many other mining supplies are available including 3-4-5-6-8-inch dredges, etc. Please write us of your equipment needs.

CUT HERE OR PHOTOCOPY